RELIGION

# A Martyr's
# Message of Hope

# A Martyr's Message of Hope

### Six Homilies
### by Archbishop Oscar Romero

## Celebration Books

### Kansas City, Missouri

The publisher gratefully acknowledges the assistance of the following translators and editors in preparing this book: Felipe Ortega, Anne Fitzgerald, Jane Stoever, Edward Wagner, Carol Meyer, Charlie Lackamp, Casilda Gomez, Art Winter and Bill Freburger. Millie Malawey typed the manuscript. A translation of the March 23, 1980 homily, by Nena Terrell and Sally Hanlon, first appeared in the May, 1980 issue of *Sojourners* (1309 L Street, N.W., Washington, DC 20005) and was consulted in translating the homily for this book.

The original Spanish homilies, as delivered by Archbishop Romero, are available on cassettes (*Un Mensaje Esperanzado de un Martir*, seven cassettes, A 1320 - A 1326, $45) from NCR Cassettes, P.O. Box 281, Kansas City, MO 64141.

Library of Congress Catalog Card No. 80-84886

ISBN: 0-934134-09-X

The publisher dedicates this translation to four American women who, like Archbishop Oscar Romero, lived and died for the people of El Salvador:

*Sister Maura Clarke, M.M.*
*Miss Jean Marie Donovan*
*Sister Ita Ford, M.M.*
*Sister Dorothy Kazel, O.S.U.*

# Contents

*Page xi*
**Glossary**


*Page 1*
**Foreword**
Moises Sandoval


*Page 4*
**The Holy Spirit:
Renewal of Our World**
May 14, 1978


*Page 29*
**An Assassination That Speaks
to Us of Resurrection**
January 21, 1979


*Page 49*
**Christ: True Shepherd—
King of All People**
July 22, 1979


*Page 75*
**The Poor: Christ's
Instrument of Liberation**
February 17, 1980

*Page 115*
**The Church: Defender
of Human Dignity**
March 23, 1980

*Page 162*
**In Death Is Our Life**
March 24, 1980

*Page 167*
**Afterword**
Rev. Virgil Elizondo

# A Martyr's
# Message of Hope

# Glossary

**ANDES.** *Asociacion Nacional de Educadores Salva-doreños,* National Association of Salvadorean Educators. A radical teachers' group, closely associated with MERS (see below).

**ANTEL.** The national telecommunications company, closely tied to rightwing interests.

**APLAR.** An electronic assembly factory, a subsidiary of Beckman Instruments of California.

**BPR.** *Bloque Popular Revolucionario,* Revolutionary Popular Bloc. One of the more radical leftist groups. Its leader, Juan Chacon, was assassinated in late November, 1980.

*Canton.* A neighborhood in an outlying district, only used to refer to poor neighborhoods.

**Christian Democrats.** A middle-of-the-road political party whose civilian leader, Napoleon Duarte, serves as a front for the military.

*Colones.* The Salvadorean currency (2.5 colones = one U.S. dollar).

Decree 114. The first land reform decree passed by the Salvadorean government.

FAPU. *Frente Accion Popular Unida,* United Popular Action Front. One of the more moderate leftist political groups.

MERS. *Movimiento Estudiantil Revolucionario Salvadoreño,* Salvadorean Revolutionary Students' Movement. A leftist group composed of high school and university students.

MNR. *Movimiento Nacional Revolucionario,* National Revolutionary Movement. A social democratic group whose self-exiled leader is Guillermo Ungo.

ORDEN. A paramilitary spy system, installed by previous dictatorships, using peasants as informers. It was technically abolished under the new government, but continues to function.

RCM. *Revolucionaria Coordinadora de Masas,* the National Revolutionary Coordinating Committee. An umbrella group of leftist organizations.

*Sandinistas.* The rebels who overthrew Somoza and who now govern Nicaragua. They are named after Cesar Agosto Sandino, a Nicaraguan rebel leader in the 1920s who fought against U.S. Marine occupation of the country.

UCA. The Jesuit-run Central American University.,

# Foreword

## Moises Sandoval

*Editor, Maryknoll Magazine*

It may be somewhat presumptuous of me to evaluate the impact of Archbishop Romero's words on El Salvador's people. I'm a North American with a mixture of Anglo-Saxon and Hispanic cultures. I did once pay a short visit to El Salvador. Of course, I've written much about El Salvador and spoken with Salvadoreans, many of them expelled from that suffering country. I have traveled much in Central America.

But I think to evaluate Archbishop Romero's impact on his people, I would have to be a Salvadorean, one who experienced the oppression and exploitation since 1932 when the military forces killed more than 30,000 persons, one who lived in the sad darkness that fell over the people since that era, one as illiterate as the majority of the Salvadorean people, one who suffered torture, the disappearance of my family, and the oppression of the security forces. If I were one of these poorest Salvadoreans, then I could say clearly and heartfeltly what I think Archbishop Romero was saying.

Of course, I don't have to be a citizen of El Salvador to know his word had a great impact. Every Sunday the San Salvador Cathedral was packed with people who came to hear his word. The congregation didn't doze during the Archbishop's long homilies (they lasted hours: one hour, an hour and a half, and even two hours). The audience was always full of life, applauding key points of the Archbishop's homily. Everywhere in that country of four and a half million, his voice was heard. On Sunday morning, people gathered in the churches to hear his words relayed by the archdiocesan radio station. In the poorest barrios, houses (hardly houses because they are cardboard) prominently displayed the Archbishop's picture. The inhabitants would say: "This is our bishop."

I once had the pleasure of meeting Archbishop Romero at the press conference he gave at Puebla during the meeting of the Latin American bishops in 1979. The Archbishop was the antithesis of the Latin American leader. That impressed me the most. The typical Latin American leader is a tall man with a tough expression and the morals of a thief; he rules by fear, not by respect. The people of El Salvador are tired of these leaders. They no longer have confidence in them and they never will. Archbishop Oscar Romero was the opposite of such a leader. He was a short man; his face was not becoming, but was very sensitive. You could imagine from his face that this man had experienced fear and suffering, but still had affection for all. Because they saw in Oscar Romero a person of the people, a neighbor, a barrio resident, perhaps therefore, the people of El Salvador could trust his word.

The homilies of Archbishop Oscar Romero, as we said, were long but they related the gospel to the people's suffering. The Archbishop spoke of the tortures the people had suffered during the week. He gave advice to the military about their duty to work for justice. He wasn't afraid to confront the authorities with the gospel. Even more, Archbishop Oscar Romero gave his people a vision of hope.

He once said in an interview with *Maryknoll* magazine that he wanted to be the voice of the voiceless. And in fact, when the Salvadoreans heard the word of their Archbishop, they heard themselves. They were like a poor and humble man who had regained his voice. Perhaps because the people heard themselves, the word of Archbishop Oscar Romero had the great impact it did not only in El Salvador but everywhere.

The Archbishop was a man who came to his people armed not with death-dealing weapons but with life-giving, hope-filled words. This word was so powerful that the oppressive authorities had to kill him, hoping to silence it forever. But the word of Archbishop Oscar Romero still resounds in the barrios, and in the actions of those who will follow his example in living not for themselves but for others. For me, that is the true significance of Archbishop Oscar Romero's words.

May 14, 1978
# The Holy Spirit:
# Renewal of Our World

*Acts 2:1-11*
*1 Corinthians 12:3-7, 12-13*
*John 20:19-23*

Beloved brothers and sisters, today is the church's birthday. This powerful day is the most beautiful one in the entire liturgical cycle that we follow step by step. Today is Pentecost; today Easter is crowned; today Christ glorified lives on in a people he calls to follow him. Christ lives today, more than ever, on Pentecost. Let this be the subject of my homily: Pentecost, birthday of the church. As good children of the church, let us be glad for a place where this holy day, the birthday of the kingdom of heaven, can be celebrated. Today is the church's birthday.

I'm going to try to develop my theme with these three ideas: the church is always an event; God's Spirit is what makes the church a new creation; and the Holy Spirit is the key to the renewal of today's world.

In the first place, I say that the church is an event, that it is good news. Twenty centuries have passed since the event we read about in the Acts of the Apostles. Likewise, 20 centuries have passed since that day when the noise of a hurricane and a shower of fiery flames fell upon Jerusalem and all the pilgrims who had come from all of the corners of the known world to be in the city for the holy day of Pentecost.

Today the church continues being the good news, an event. The church is always a community experience that leads people to listen to the wonders of the Lord and, in their evangelical role as Christ's faithful followers, to denounce the sin of the world wherever it is found. The church is always good news because as God's people we always need to hear his wonders. People—above all the poorest, those who suffer the most, those who seem to live without hope—always need to hear of the benevolence of the Spirit who inspires their hope and denounces the injustices that oppress them.

Who could have told me that on this day of Pentecost in 1978 I would be like the hurricane in Jerusalem, attracting the attention of such a large audience, particularly the supreme court of justice? Because of publicity throughout the republic, a lot of interest has been generated regarding this day of Pentecost in the cathedral of San Salvador. Because of the inquiry of the supreme court of justice, I know that there is great expectation about what I have to say.

For the time being, I want to tell you that the supreme court has been God's sign today in attracting the people's attention. By being interested in what the church has to say, the court is serving us, just as the wind and fiery flames served God's purpose at Pentecost.

May the church always have Pentecost, and may she always recognize the Holy Spirit's beauty. When the church stops holding its doors open to the divine truth that Christ gave it on this day and instead expects to nourish you through the fragile forces of this land's power or wealth, then the church stops being that good news.

The church will be forever beautiful, tremendously young and attractive, as long as it remains faithful to the Spirit that illuminates it through its communities, its shepherds and its own life. Thanks be to God, the church in our archdiocese tries to be faithful to that Spirit. For that reason, we should be grateful to the Lord on this Pentecost day. We celebrate Pentecost today, Sunday, May 14, 1978, but the reality of this feast continues to live on amid pain, the way of the cross, and the joys of Easter.

A profound joy lives in the hearts of our communities' shepherds. It is here that Pentecost lives in our archdiocese. To the priests, the precious religious communities, all of the institutions that glory in the name Catholic (such as the schools, the associations, the communities, etc.) and even more, all of you Christians beyond the boundaries of Catholicism who have shown yourselves united in trying to be evangelical for Christ's church that extends throughout the four districts of our archdiocese—I only want to say to you, brothers and sisters, Catholics and Christians, "Let us try to be faithful to the Holy Spirit; let us try to be the perfect reflection of the Holy Spirit; before all else let us have hope in God's Spirit and be faithful to the holiness of that

Spirit which permeates God's kingdom on earth." I
congratulate all of those communities, pastors, catechists, celebrants of the word, and others who collaborate daily with God's Spirit to further renew the beauty
of our archdiocese. You genuinely reflect the glorious
abundance, the light, the fire, the wind, the hurricane
of the Holy Spirit.

My second point is this: the Spirit makes the church a
new creation. Now let's consider the gospel passage in
which Christ, having risen from the dead on Easter,
opens the door to the upper room and enters into the
midst of his disciples. They were frightened of the Jews
and persecution, and so, were hiding. Christ says to
them with the serenity of one whose life is already over,
"Peace be unto you." The solemn gesture where Christ
—who is both man and God—blows upon the faces of
his apostles reminds us of the incident recorded in the
Bible's first page where God created humanity in his
shape and image and likeness by blowing upon the clay
of the earth to give it the spirit of life.

One might say that Christ is the creator forming a
new creation with the "clay" of human flesh. He says,
"Just as my Father filled me, so I have endowed you to
receive the Holy Spirit." Those who pardon sin are
themselves pardoned, and those who stay in sin remain
behind. We are reminded of Adam, who fell to his knees
to pray after he awoke from the first dream of humanity
and saw the breath of God reflected in his own person.
With his intelligence, he understood the wonder of creation and fell to his knees to make the first such gesture
before God. So it seems to me that the consciences of the

apostles—simple people, cowards hidden for fear of persecution—were struck when they received Christ's Spirit in the same way that Adam was touched by God's Spirit when he first awoke.

The gospel of St. John unites Christ's resurrection and Pentecost as a single act of the Lord because the two holy days, separated by 50 days in our liturgical year, are no more than a single reality. This reality is the glorification of Christ. It is Christ, both human and divine, becoming a creator and shaping the apostles as a new creation on earth. So it is that the apostles became new Adams, not with the simple and natural life that the creator gave them but with the life of the Holy Spirit that comes from God and is conveyed to the church.

Open your eyes, confused ones, and feel God's power in you. Christ's mission to renew the world is in your hands, as is God's power to pardon. Easter is in the hands of that part of the world called the church, which Christ created. He made the church his gift of life to all humanity. It is the source, the yeast, the ferment, the light of the world.

This is the Easter creation. Pentecost is the birthday of the church because on this day it was born. The church is that group of people, believers in Christ, that receives Christ's Spirit from the messiah's omnipotent breath. They receive the redeemer's power to convert everyone into messiahs and redeemers.

Dear Christians, we are all the new creation. The world will not be renewed without us. We are responsible for the renovation of the world. Since the day of his resurrection, Christ's kingdom has been in the midst of humanity. The kingdom of God is already being built on this earth. To preach a church with only the hope of an afterlife is to falsify the kingdom of God. The kingdom that Christ preached and established is precisely that creation of his breath. It is made up of those pilgrims who traverse the earth with the responsibility of transforming history into the kingdom of God. We do not aspire to temporal power. Rather, in the face of the abuses and undesirability of this power, these pilgrims look to the church, which has the great responsibility to sanctify all human institutions. The church need not do away with power or money in order to rid the world of idols. The church only needs hearts converted to Christ, purified like clean vessels so that the new life Christ initiated might descend upon them.

In the sense of that resurrection and Pentecost of 20 centuries ago, the church continues to be good news and to celebrate its birthday year after year. Today on Pentecost, we rejoice once again in the life of the church. In 1978, we can say that the universal church— to which this beautiful church in my archdiocese is joined—celebrating its birthday and life, is so young, so beautiful, so handsome, broader, stronger and more faithful to the Spirit, blessed be God. Brothers and sisters, it is worth the effort to belong to this new creation and to allow ourselves to be filled with the strength of the Spirit that identifies us with Christ's mission—one that brings peace, destroys sin and makes humanity just.

If we had the time, this would be a great opportunity

to give a beautiful catechesis about the Spirit of Yahweh, the Spirit of God, that we continue to discover in the pages of the Bible. In Hebrew, the original biblical word for spirit is *ruah;* in Greek, it is *pneuma;* and in our Castilian, it is *espíritu.* What is the Bible telling us with the word *ruah* which God utters for the first time over the clay that he is about to mold into humankind? From the outset, it means life, life from God conveyed to the human being.

As you know, the Bible has many anthropomorphic expressions. That is to say, God and people are often compared. In its likening of God to humans, many times the Bible mentions this *ruah*, this breath of God, his Spirit, his exhalation. As a life-giving power which transforms sin into goodness God's breath at times becomes a hurricane; the Bible says God is breathing strongly. At other times, it is a soft breeze; then, the Bible describes it as God's gentle Spirit, soft as a breeze. But the creator, the Spirit, is always a powerful force. It is called "blessed" just as it is called "God's holy arm." The latter is an anthropomorphic expression because in reality God has no arm. The Bible speaks of God's holy arm to mean his power. It also speaks of the holy breath of God—*espíritu, ruah, pneuma*—meaning an attraction to God on a natural level. When Christ came, he raised the spirit to a supernatural level. The entire literature of the New Testament, having inherited all of that rich tradition on the Spirit of God, raises its meaning to include the revelation of Christ. He told us that the Spirit of God is not simply a breath but also a person, the third person of that most blessed Trinity in which the Father eternally engenders a Son. They love one another so deeply that their being is breathed forth and speaks to us of a profoundly personal love. The Spirit of God is love, the third person of the most holy Trinity. In theology, this is called "hypostasis." That is to say, the Spirit is like a person, a person like the Father, like the Son. And so, the Holy Spirit was sent in Christ, who was glorified as testimony that God had accepted his redemption and would come to take up all believers. "If I do not go," Christ told his apostles at the last supper, "I will not be able to send you the other consoler and mediator."

See how Christ speaks of his other being, of his "Godness," as divine, as loving, as powerful and as true as himself. We no longer see Christ as the person of God embodied as a human being, walking the roads of the earth. But along the earth's roadways, we will find many men and women who follow Christ through the Holy Spirit and are guided by the divine force of his redemption. This is because the Spirit that Christ sent from his heart and from God the Father to this church, who moves about the earth, is the other counselor, the one who preaches through ministers, the one who continues being life for the church.

Brothers and sisters, if I had the time, I would analyze paragraph four of the *Dogmatic Constitution on the Church* from the Second Vatican Council. I invite those Catholics who have taken the time to study the council documents to look at the dogmatic constitution, *Lumen Gentium*, which speaks about the church. Paragraph four talks of the Holy Spirit's action within the church. You can see there how the council makes a very beautiful synthesis of the function of the Holy Spirit in the church. The council tells us that the Holy Spirit leads the church to the fullness of truth and renews her through the holiness of her people. It also says that the Holy Spirit enriches the church through its gifts and charisms.

In today's second reading, St. Paul gave us another fine example of the work of the Holy Spirit among humanity, in all of the church's communities. This function of the Holy Spirit is to give various vocations and hierarchical and charismatic gifts. It is the one that gives strength and perseverance to those fulfilling the church's mission in spite of all their tribulations. For that reason, on this Pentecost we have really pleaded for the strength of the Spirit so that the church—especially in the archdiocese of San Salvador—might have many more priests, religious, catechists, committed laity and communities that sincerely choose to be guided by the power of the Holy Spirit.

Whatever has been said is enough as long as we remain very strong in our faith, hope and paschal joy. Let us realize we have the good fortune to belong to this church that functions in the world as an effective sign of the new creation. As Catholics who truly have faith in the Holy Spirit, let us give ourselves to the task of renovating the world and building our country anew. In light of the sins of El Salvador and her institutions, part of our mission must also be to destroy sin and forge the kingdom of God in its stead. This we will do if we are truly a people who have been touched by the

Holy Spirit. The Catholic Salvadorean must be a source of renewal if the church is to be the instrument of the Spirit, the source of redemption. If the church is supposed to shape all her followers into authentic liberators of freedom from sin, if she is to sincerely promote life through God's grace and make God's children into citizens of heaven, then we all must do our part to help.

Let us not allow this country, so gloriously named after the divine Savior, to be destroyed. The entire world, like our own country, might be named after the divine Savior because all who believe in Christ are an extension of his divine salvation. Because of our baptism, our commitment to Christ, our gospel, let us Salvadoreans make a major pledge, a truly faithful promise in spite of all that we already have to do, to be driven by the Spirit. All of us sense the Holy Spirit, but not all of us are faithful to him. Our cowardices reproach us, and yet we are unable to overcome them. We know that the Holy Spirit blows strongly to create brave people, but we are still cowards and even give that spirit of cowardice to others. And we lie even though Christ is the spirit of truth. Those who have received the Holy Spirit and yet rebuff him should not call themselves Christians because they only live by lies, injustice, slander, violence and all those things that repress the Spirit's life. How I wish our church could be the new creation in the midst of all of the terrible events of our history!

Finally, sisters and brothers, my third thought is that

the Holy Spirit renews our present world. And on this glorious Pentecost in 1978 I am going to concretize this idea through three specific events.

The first event was the confirmation of the youth last night. Two hundred young people filled this cathedral on the eve of Pentecost. In the magnificent sacrament of confirmation, they stood with their godparents and mothers and fathers and promised to be open to the Holy Spirit and faithful to his inspiration. As the ceremony was ending, a young man stood in this same pulpit from which I now preach and delivered a very moving message to the youth. I want to stress his two big challenges to them.

First he called all youth, mainly the 200 who were confirmed last night, to continue gathering in order to meditate on God's word and to organize small reflection groups. Brothers and sisters, we already know the danger this poses in our situation. The study of our religion and reflection on God's word becomes controversial when it has these goals: to lead others to an awareness of God's word, to speak against cowardice, and to call for justice and true order rather than docile conformity and outrageous abuse. To be gathered around God's word to pray and meditate upon it is not a subversive activity but a constructive one. The youth committed themselves to reflect on the word of God in that way.

The other call voiced by that young man was this—that, from this night onward, the youth who were confirmed in the cathedral of San Salvador extend an open invitation and challenge to all youth in the archdiocese. The challenge is that all young people begin now to prepare themselves for a youth celebration of Easter on Holy Saturday night of 1979. The challenge is that the youth of El Salvador proclaim that Christ lives and is risen. The best argument for everlasting life is not the empty tomb but rather the lives of the young who embody Christ's enthusiasm, joy, sincerity and spirit of renewal.

For me, this action of the youth has been the most beautiful gift the Holy Spirit has given us this Pentecost in 1978. I want to congratulate and thank the Catholic schools, the parishes and the communities that collaborated on this beautiful project, the youths' confirmation.

These young people made real our desire that confirmation not be a sacrament for children unaware of its significance; rather, it has to be a sacrament for young people who are aware of the Spirit of Christ. So, after the first Sunday of Advent—that is to say, from November and December of this year—little children will no longer be allowed to be confirmed. My brothers and sisters, try to understand. Caring for those children is quite different from their being confirmed without realizing what it means to be confirmed. They are altogether distinct from the youth confirmed last night who sense the struggle of new passions and circumstances in the world, and as baptized children of God, understand the arrival of adolescence and the need for added strength from the Holy Spirit. Our Pentecost was a grand event because 200 youths consciously opened their hands and hearts to say, "Come, Holy Spirit, fill up the joy of our youthfulness!"

The second thing that I want to point out is that this Pentecost is the day of the seminary. This special day, which unites us Salvadoreans, ought to move us to reflect seriously on sending more than mere greetings of admiration to the young men who have answered God's call to the priesthood at a time when being a priest means being either crazy or heroic. There can be no middle ground. Mediocre priests, halfway priests, priests who compromise with God and the devil do not have authentic vocations. We greet and admire the young men who fill the seminary today. Many of them are committed to the priesthood because they long for a grand heroism. For them it is worth the effort to be protagonists and heroes with Christ, to preach the kingdom in the midst of so many worldly idolatries through his spirit of strength. My brothers and sisters, the seminary's tremendous contribution concerns all of us. San José de la Montaña is not just a cement monument. . . .

All the people in the diocese ought to unite as a symbol of hope, aiding the seminary with prayers and moral support, so our youth do not become discouraged. We should be concerned about them and ask how they are doing, and tell them we look forward to their ministry. Above all, brothers and sisters, we must understand that in a time of such profound changes—as a seminarian was telling us here before mass—the seminarian today cannot embody the old traditions without becoming a leader. The seminary is not a school for guerrillas even if some youth leave it to take up arms. The seminary is a school for the promotion of young men, for the development of young priests that today's people so desperately need. Its aim is to form men of prayer who are very committed to God. Such men know as well how to be one with the people, to be in their midst, serving as their voice, feeling united with them and knowing their anxieties as well as their hopes. Thanks be to God, these are the seminarians that San José de la Montaña nourishes today.

Also, my people, let us understand the humble conditions of the families from which the majority of these vocations come. What these future priests need is not charity, but rather a show of responsibility by the entire people of God. If there are families that have given up their sons to the priesthood in spite of being very poor, then it is only just that other families to whom God has not given a vocation be generous in helping the seminary.

Brothers and sisters, today when one tries to become a priest and meets so many obstacles and does not have the financial means, it matters not. Our power rests in the Holy Spirit who calls for help from the generous people who make it possible to maintain a seminary full of vocations.

Now I want to honor and congratulate the staff of young priests, representing the universal church, that educates these young men so well. I would like the people to know them so they might realize that these priests who shape our future clergy are guilty of none of the false accusations that are often made to discredit the work of the seminary. I also want to pay tribute to the seminary's excellence and express my admiration and profound gratitude. Father Ladislao Segura, an unforgettable figure to many, was brought to the seminary after his death. In a gesture of profound gratitude, his corpse was buried before the Blessed Sacrament and the statue of Mary, where the seminarians pray and watch over it. There he will always be in prayer. He was a man consumed by life, and so we might speak of his life as a total priestly existence. Hidden like a violet, largely unnoticed in its beauty, his life was one of service to this seminary apostolate.

Finally, my brothers and sisters, there is a third thing to note this Pentecost: we are called to an evangelical proclamation of justice in the midst of our country's harsh realities.

Fifteen days ago, I was speaking these precise words in this same place. Brothers and sisters, we must not forget that a group of lawyers are fighting for amnesty, and publishing their reasons for asking mercy on behalf of so many who wind up in the prisons. These same lawyers also denounce anomalies in the proceedings of the main penal court where the judge does not allow the lawyers to enter with their defendants. And yet the National Guard's presence is allowed, which terrifies the accused, who often show signs of being tortured. Any judge who does not denounce this torture but instead ignores it, is not a just judge in the eyes of his prisoner.

Dear people, I think that in the face of these injustices which are witnessed all around us in the high courts and in many local courtrooms, we have to conclude this: judges are bribed. What is the supreme court doing about this? Where is the action of this transcendent, democratic power that ought to be above all other powers calling for justice from those who trample upon it?

I believe that a big part of our country's uneasiness is due to the fact that the president and the supreme court of justice do not demand with any firmness that the courts of justice, the judges and all of the administrators of that holy word "justice" truly be agents of justice!

I want to congratulate the Christian and non-Christian lawyers for the great sense of justice with which they are putting their fingers on a sore spot. God willing, may all of our lawyers truly be the hope for a justice that is so absent in our situation. This is what I said 15 days ago that provoked the secretary of the supreme court of justice to respectfully ask me to reveal the names of those venal judges to whom I had referred in the homily in question. I want to clarify some things about the communique sent to me, especially considering the possible confusion among the people brought on by the publications of the supreme court of justice and by commentaries from the national press.

Above all, I am happy and grateful for the opportunity the supreme court of justice is offering me to amplify what I said in my homily given on April 30th of this year at mass in the cathedral. I am overjoyed because at last the supreme court of justice is publicly declaring its intention to begin rectifying what is wrong with that supreme power which is so vitally important to peace in our country. The court is finally acting after having denounced these abuses for so long.

Second, the supreme court's courteous note to me is not a legal summons, since it is not addressed to me in any legal way. Therefore, my answer is a spontaneous reaffirmation of my pastoral commitment to the defense of justice, truth and the people.

Furthermore, I tell you that this most respectful note from the secretary of the supreme court of justice has mutilated the meaning and changed the essence of my original message. Clearly, he is trying to compel me to reveal the names of the mercenary judges to whom I referred at that time. But since I did not use the term "venal" textually, as quoted in the note, if I undoubtedly mentioned in my homily judges who sell themselves, then it refers to a term that is merely incidental to the entire context of my message. That is, I denounced irregularities much broader than those that pertain to the entire system of judicial administration. To place exclusive emphasis on that incidental term without mentioning the general context which frames it is an illogical and unjust way of deciding that it suggests something more than it does.

By doing that, the supreme court of justice gives the impression that it wants to conceal or distract public opinion from the central focus of my message, which I now repeat. My message was and continues to be the denunciation of a social ill rooted in institutions and procedures that fall under the responsibility of that honorable tribunal, the supreme court of justice.

Third, apart from this, it is a well-known fact that proof of the venal acts which the supreme court wants me to produce is most difficult to come up with. The simple reason for this is that the offenses involve officials who are themselves corrupt, just like those who buy them and all of those who collaborate in the negotiations. For that reason, it remains highly unlikely that anyone who has been mixed up in such acts would want to testify against the others involved.

Fourth, I also ought to clarify that when I deliver homilies, my perspective as pastor is a theological one, concerned about justice. I have often reiterated that the message and the attitude of the church go beyond the realms of human dealings or of politics. Rather, the message springs from an evangelical concern that obligates the church to denounce sin wherever it might be found. It is most important that I as pastor courageously point out where those anomalies come from that cause the outcries of a people oppressed by sin and the world's injustices. It would be wise for the supreme court of justice to note that in an authentic democracy the supreme court watches over compliance with the laws, denounces abuses by the greatest powers of the state, carries out the law, and demands accountability. The note that I was honored to receive expressed this so eloquently.

I am not the one designated to name those whom the supreme court can investigate. Other groups are doing this kind of thing, for instance, the mothers and relatives of political prisoners, the exiled, and those who have disappeared. So many denunciations of venality have been publicized by responsible means of social communication, both here and abroad. Aside from this, I believe from my theological perspective that a mercenary attitude fills any public official who receives a salary from the people to administer justice and instead becomes an accomplice to injustice and is motivated by sinful gratifications. Let me just say that one can investigate this phenomenon with greater ease if they have a sense of mission and serious duty, along with the necessary tools to do so.

But fifth, without a doubt something far more serious than mercenary activity occurs when others show outright scorn for the obligations of the honorable supreme court of justice which the political constitution imposes upon it and which all of the court's members have been obligated to carry out. That honorable court has not remedied situations so contrary to public freedom and human rights, whose defense constitutes its highest mission. We must deal with the fact that the fundamental rights of the Salvadorean people are trampled upon day to day without any institution denouncing the outrages and moving sincerely and effectively to change the situation.

The eighth article of the human rights document is sacred. It says that each person has the right to effective recourse before the responsible national courts of justice that defend them against acts that violate their fundamental rights acknowledged by the constitution or by the law. Specifically, in our country article 164 of the constitution says that each person has the right to habeas corpus before the supreme court of justice or the lower court when any authority or individual illegally obstructs their freedom. Several justices, honest and valiant, have informed the supreme court about the impossibility of finding within the security forces the help that they need to carry out their sacred constitutional mission.

In article 164, the political constitution reads, "No one can be deprived of their life, liberty, property or possessions without having been heard previously and duly investigated in accordance with the laws, nor can they be indicted twice for the same reason." I would like to point out that many mothers and wives of people who have disappeared have come to us. This has been an especially painful situation for me. Some people have disappeared under circumstances that are common knowledge to all Salvadoreans, others in situations so unique that people presume the viciousness of the disappearances. Several mothers, wives and children have crossed the entire country from end to end bearing the sad ordeal of searching for their loved ones without finding any answers. We can be certain that there are about 80 families with some member who has been seized without having been assigned to any court up to this point. In light of this most serious situation which daily tears the hearts of these mothers, wives and children, I stress one particular point of the new article of the declaration of human rights. And it is this: no one can be arbitrarily detained, arrested or banished.

Article 13 of the universal declaration of human rights says that every person has the right to leave any country, including their own, and to return to their country. I also recall this right being stated in the constitution. It protects all Salvadoreans who find themselves in agonizing exile. Article 164 of the constitution officially declares that no Salvadorean can be expatriated or forbidden entry into the republic or denied their passport or other documents of identification for reentry. In spite of this, protests of those Salvadoreans who cannot enter the country are given little attention.

Article 162 of the constitution says that each person has the right to direct petitions to the legally established authorities so that their grievances might be resolved and the result made known. We must remember that several lawyers, a group concerned with the exercise of basic rights, have respectively presented a petition of amnesty for all those people mixed up in the events at San Pedro Perulapan. They also submitted an appeal questioning the constitutionality of the law of defense and the guarantee of public order. Several weeks have passed since their pleadings, and as yet we have not received any resolutions from those responsible for them.

The press has revealed several anomalous situations which leave the people tremendously uneasy. These revelations denounce both administrative and judicial officials. And yet in spite of the common knowledge of these irregularities we have not noticed any real interest on the part of the responsible authorities. I do not intend to specify details concerning these situations. I am thoroughly convinced that if there truly existed a social conscience within the administration of public affairs, then these acts would be investigated exhaustively, and the end result would be the achievement of a truly authentic social well-being such as we had before.

As I have said, the universal declaration of human rights, as well as our fundamental law, is consecrated in the sacred right to freedom which has been violated in many different ways. No power, no authority, no civil servant should be able to dictate orders of detention or imprisonment unless they are in compliance with the law. Furthermore, these orders must always be written. To the contrary, there are people who are seized by the security forces, placed at the disposal of the courts, and held more than eight days without constitutional directives being observed. There are people who have been illegally detained and held by the security forces for over 30 days. Such situations are common knowledge, recounted in news releases about such painful events as those that took place in Aguilares, El Paisnal, San Pedro Perulapan and San Marcos Lenpa. I know perfectly well that there are legal limits which the security forces are obligated to observe in guarding prisoners. I also know that there are penal constraints so that this custody may not be violent or terrifying to the person detained. And yet how many prisoners have appeared before the courts with clear signs of poor treatment!

In keeping with article 191 of our constitution, workers have the right to associate freely in defense of their own interest in forming trade unions. This initial formation of syndicates and this unionization in defense of workers' interests are supported by articles 23 and 24 of the human rights manifesto. This manifesto is itself weak in many ways, especially in restricting the freedom of labor leaders and subtly granting concessions to those workers who reject the union organization. Because of this, we should not support the right of workers to strike, as it is set out in article 192 of the political constitution. This measure has been used as a last resort by the Salvadorean worker, and the authorities have trampled upon and twisted it without hesitation. It is said that the majority of strikes are subversive and that they are based on false international standards. This measure is being utilized by the workers as a legal means to defend collective labor contracts, salaries and vacation days recognized in the labor laws and to protect their professional interests. This complies with the universal declaration of human rights and with our own constitution. Forming unions is made sacred as a social right. Therefore, it is impossible to understand all of the inconveniences, hindrances and obstacles that the farm worker faces daily in carrying out that basic right.

Sixth and finally, in the face of these situations that are common knowledge it seems to us that judicial power has generally been exercised in intervention, as I illustrated in the homily alluded to. This is fundamental and important. I ask, where is the transcendent role of this power in a democracy that ought to value and call for justice from all those who trample upon it? As pastor of a people that suffers injustice, I believe that it is my duty to make this denunciation which draws its inspiration from a positive spirit of fraternal correction and not from a malicious spirit of backbiting. The gospel is vital to what I am compelled to confront, namely the judicial process and the prison system, because all that is being done with them seems to add more injustice.

I want to finish by sincerely thanking countless persons, especially the kind professionals and law students, who have touched me by making themselves jointly liable in this open concern for justice in our country. Above all, I am grateful because this collaboration is a positive construction of peace. Well, my brothers and sisters, this church of the Holy Spirit has been proclaimed ever since the ancient times of the prophet Isaiah. And today with the renewed youthfulness of this Pentecost in 1978, I repeat that in the midst of the dramatic reality of our people peace can only be the product of justice, and the work of justice is only peace (Isaiah 32:17).

January 21, 1979
# An Assassination that Speaks to Us of Resurrection

Jonah 3:1-5, 10
1 Corinthians 7:29-31
Mark 1:14-20

*San Salvador's Archbishop Oscar A. Romero gave this homily at the funeral of a priest and four youths, all killed by San Salvador's National Guard. Dr. Jorge Lara-Braud represented the World Council of Churches and the National Council of Churches of the United States. Before the homily, Dr. Lara-Braud extended his sympathy to the Salvadorean people. This is a portion of what he said:*

*"I can hear Father Octavio Ortiz Luna from eternity, where there is no more death or weeping, telling each one of us, his surviving brothers and sisters: 'Now I take joy in what I suffer for you and make up what is lacking in the sufferings of Christ in my body for the good of his body, the church.'*

*" . . . In representing my adopted country, the United States of America, and the Christians of my adopted country, I beg your forgiveness, my Salvadorean brothers and sisters, for the measure in which my*

*country aids a social structure that creates poverty and rewards oppressors.*

*"The World Council of Churches and the National Council of Churches join you in your sorrow. Moreover, they also join you in that subversive joy that can say the assassins have not really killed Octavio Ortiz Luna and his brothers; they have not really assassinated them; they have given them life eternal."*

*Archbishop Romero then delivered this homily.*

Beloved brother priests: Thank you for coming here to express your solidarity, even though you had to sacrifice your regular Sunday schedule. This solemn time makes us feel so strongly our common brotherhood!

Thanks, also, to our brother pastor Jorge Lara-Braud, for his ecumenical message. He gives us strength in our pilgrimage of trying to be faithful to the gospel that unites us all—Protestants, Orthodox or Catholics—who seek to faithfully interpret the gospel in these days of contrary influences.

We meet today surrounded by the corpses of our highly esteemed brother priest, Father Octavio Ortiz, and the four youths who died with him, killed by gunshots: Angel Morales, Jorge Alberto Gomez, Roberto Orellana and David Alberto Caballeros.

Today the Catholic community adopts ecumenical and eschatological perspectives. The multitude that fills the cathedral and the park extends itself, by radio, to almost all of the republic and beyond the diocese and the motherland. We sense that we are united in faith and hope with all the people of God on pilgrimage in all the countries of the world.

I believe, brothers and sisters, that on very few occasions can one feel the reality of the Sunday mass as fully as we do today. The Second Vatican Council defined the Sunday celebration as an "apostolic tradition that took its origin from the very day of the resurrection. The church celebrates the paschal mystery—death/resurrection—every eighth day, which day is appropriately called the Lord's day or Sunday. For on this day Christ's faithful are bound to come together into one place. They should listen to the word of God and take part in the eucharist, thus calling to mind the passion, resurrection and glory of the Lord Jesus, and giving thanks to God who has begotten them again, through the resurrection of Christ from the dead, unto a living hope" (*Constitution on the Sacred Liturgy,* no. 106).

This hope and this participation in the death and resurrection of Christ are our painful reality today. We gather around these corpses that themselves preach the message of the three readings we have just heard.

Before reflecting upon those readings, I want to dwell upon you who form the multitude. You have come from different sections of the diocese and the motherland. The cathedral is too small for all of you who have invaded it with your love and faith, and thus it had to be expanded into the street.

We feel that this liturgy on earth, this mass in the cathedral, this communion, unites us with the liturgy of heaven. We meet in the presence of these corpses but we know these men are not dead but are pilgrims about to reach true life. We who are still a pilgrim community are called to trust even more in that hope which is already great in all our hearts. This is an ecclesial community that can speak out about the incidents occurring in our country, as it has been speaking out about them every week.

What eager longing our continent feels before the pope's arrival in Mexico and the meeting at Puebla. My heart is divided as I await this visit. I sincerely desire to go and meet with the pope and with my brother bishops from the continent. I will not go for pleasure, nor for rest, but in the quest to better serve the diocese, and in the desire to share the unfathomable riches of our archdiocese. These riches are great: they are you; they are your communities; they are your faith; they are your suffering; they are your persecution.

I feel what St. Paul said: "I want to stay with you in so painful and dangerous an hour" for our church. But on the other hand, I feel the need to take all these concerns so that they may be felt in Puebla and from there may be carried to the borders of the continent and to the whole world. And even though I am a pastor, I am weak, and a humble Christian, and I feel that my faith will be made robust through contact with the Roman pontiff.

Thus, brothers and sisters, I ask your permission to leave you orphans for a while so that I may take your riches to Puebla and bring back the pope's strength and that of my brother bishops who will meet there. I beg your prayers. I want to represent the archdiocese in prayer. No one should cease praying! Today we have five new intercessors in heaven who love this diocese. To serve her better, they were preparing themselves in a community experience when they met death. Let us pray then that Puebla may be what America and all the world hopes for.

Let me share something beautiful! I'd like to think the following telegram reflects your sentiments, dearest brothers and sisters. It was sent to me with a fraternal sign of affection from Father Alex Poprawa, of Flores, Chalatenango. It said, "A poor old woman had a mass offered that you have a good journey to Mexico, Archbishop. I am very happy at her profound faith. Greetings." Just as I rely on this dear old woman in prayer, I want to be able to count on the prayers of all who make up the church of the archdiocese.

I also want to give you one bit of advice: Be careful of the manipulation done to the news! Be very careful! Puebla is becoming a tasty morsel for those who distort the truth.

We have seen the brutal misrepresentation of the facts we are lamenting this morning. There are reasons to fear that so sacred an act as the pope's visit, one so full of hope, will be ruined by the avaricious interests of those controlling our political system, our economy and our public communications systems. Let us be above all of that. Let us try to live the true message of Puebla which we will be in charge of transmitting by our own means of public communication.

The people who are meeting here, next to the cathedral, are here for the Octave of Church Unity, of which we have just been reminded by our esteemed brother Jorge Lara-Braud. All the Catholic and Protestant churches are hoping and praying for union.

Likewise, they are praying that they will not allow any manipulation of the gospel. Rather, they know the gospel is not to be a plaything of politics, nor of convenience, but must be preserved in its full integrity. Thus it will be capable of denouncing all which clouds its authentic message. We shall continue to seek with our Protestant brothers and sisters a gospel that will truly be at the service of our nation which is suffering so much.

I want to express, also, at this time of sorrow, our sympathy to two brother priests: Father Gabriel Rodriguez, who mourns the death of his father, and Father Porfirio Martinez, from the diocese of San Vincente, who grieves over the assassination of his brother, Gilbert, near San Francisco, Chinameca.

I am pleased with you in this community for the spirit of sharing you have tried to develop. This is expressed by a Christian from one of our communities, Marcos Luis Maldonado, who wrote us from New York. He sent us 100 colones, and said, "This is a small contribution for the people who are most in need at this time in my country, sent with all my concern and gained with the sweat of my brow. In order to survive I have had to be separated from my loved ones and my motherland, which is what I least want during this Christmas season."

The church gathered together here also receives strong support from a great prelate of South America, Bishop Leonidas Proana, of Rio Bamba, Ecuador. Yesterday I received a letter from him, saying:

"We are following with interest the painful events in El Salvador. We stand beside you and all Christians who suffer for the sake of the gospel. I hope we will be able to see each other at the Puebla conference and comfort each other in our struggle to help our people become the people of God, marching toward complete liberation."

I cannot refrain from describing the facts other sources have not described, facts that you shall be able to follow by listening to our own public communications system. These facts are the very ones that bring us together here from the various regions of our archdiocese: the facts surrounding the bloody and painful case of Octavio Ortiz Luna.

The diocese declares that the official communique which the public commuinications media published, concerning this case is false from beginning to end. Our own means of public communication are already pointing out, one by one, all those false charges that the official communique states in so few lines. We trust our declaration will safeguard the faith of the motherland.

Thanks be to God, we rely on the testimony of many who survived the tragedy to reconstruct the truth. They were taken to prison by the National Guard. And thanks be to God, then, that what happened to our poor brother Ernesto Barrera did not occur in the case of

Octavio Ortiz. Ernesto Barrera was the only one who could have revealed the truth about the tragedy he witnessed, but he was assassinated by the same security agents involved in that tragedy so there would be no surviving witnesses.

Concerning the case of Octavio Ortiz, here is the first testimony that we have on hand:

"  . . . This day, at seven in the morning, when I was still sleeping . . . ."

Sleeping! Keep in mind all these details. The killings occurred at a convention of youths regarding Christian initiation. They were not armed men seeking to defend themselves; they were asleep.

"  . . . In the wing of the retreat house used for Christian groups, the place called 'The Awakening' . . . , property located in San Antonio de Abad that belongs to San Salvador's archbishop . . . ."

To those of you who do not know this house, I extend the invitation to get to know it, so you may see it does not resemble military quarters, nor does it have the purpose of forming guerrillas. Instead, for many years it has served to form Christian groups through teaching the fundamentals of the gospel, which naturally are fundamentals very dangerous to follow in our time.

The testimony continues: "  . . . Many uniformed members of the National Police and Guard violently entered this place firing their guns. A large green vehicle, called a military tank, along with a military jeep, broke into the center of the retreat house, coming into the central patio.

"I was at this center. Along with Father Octavio Ortiz Luna, a Catholic priest, and 10 other youths, I was directing a Christian Initiation Encounter for 28 male youths, whose ages range from 12 to 20. The exclusive purpose of that place is Christian formation; it has never been used for other types of meetings in which there is conspiracy against the state, nor for meetings supporting anarchical doctrines against public order.

"In the study session called 'Christian Initiation Encounter for Youth,' which had begun on Friday the 19th of this month at 5 p.m., Catholic hymn books were used. The only instruments there were musical instruments, such as guitars. None of the participants possessed firearms of any sort.

"Before being captured by uniformed members of the National Police, I was able to see that exactly in front of the offices, at the entryway to the offices and practically at the principal entrance, Father Octavio Ortiz was lying on the ground in a pool of blood, bleeding from the head.

"The police agents transported me along with one of the directors of the Christian formation team in a radio patrol car to the headquarters of the National Guard where we were interrogated and where I made known all that I have said up until this moment in this document."

During the interrogation, questions were asked about the bishop, namely, whether it was true that he was trying to sow the seeds of subversion in such centers.

This community of our archdiocese, that will be collecting other testimonies, thanks be to God, wants to make clear the contrast between the government's version of the story—full of lies—and the witnesses' version—the truth as they lived it.

It is fitting to draw some conclusions:

a) That our security corps is incapable of recognizing its errors. Instead, they make them more grave by falsifying the truth with slander. Thus they are damaging day by day the credibility of our government and our public means of communication, obliging us to resort to international organizations and publications because we no longer believe in the justice and truth of our own public media.

b) That it is increasingly urgent that our country's corrupt security system be purified. A ray of hope appeared when a certain security corps seemed to be changing its direction. That hope is waning because of the brutality we are denouncing today.

c) That one more time the wickedness and cruelty of the Law of Guarantee and Political Order have been verified. Through this law, suspicions become justifications for violating the liberty and the life of Salvadoreans.

d) That we have had enough! We say this not with pessimism but with great optimism; we place our trust in the strength of our noble nation. The country is saturated with brutality. We must return to reflection, and as rational beings search out the causes of our malady. Then we will, without fear, make the bold changes our society so urgently needs.

e) Finally, that those who ordered and those who accomplished the assassination of Father Octavio Ortiz, have incurred canonical excommunication, which in this case can be nothing else: excommunication from the church, blessed be God, at which many laugh. Perhaps this will make them ponder their deed. This church is identified with the people. The rejection by the people themselves ratifies the excommunication. But the church, like a mother, in her severity does not forget mercy. As she prays for the eternal repose of the victims and the consolation of the families that mourn, she also asks and hopes for the conversion of the assassins.

The bodies of Father Octavio Ortiz Luna, and the four youths killed with him yesterday preach to us in paschal terms.

This is our church! We must listen to the four bodies of the young men under the direction of Father Ortiz and above all to the body of Father Ortiz. In the silence of death, they bring us a transcendent message.

Let me give a brief biography of Father Octavio Ortiz Luna. A young priest, born not long ago on March 22, 1944, in a hamlet of Cacaopera, in the state of Morazan. Father Ortiz maintained the simplicity of a field hand. He knew the greatness of people is not in appearances but in truth. His parents, Don Alejandro

Ortiz and Dona Exaltacion Luna, both also shining examples of faithful fieldworkers, are here among us. To them, as to the parents of the deceased youths, we extend our condolences.

Father Ortiz came to study in our San Jose de la Montana seminary. I had the honor of being the bishop that ordained him a priest. He is the reward of my episcopate! His first assignment was in the community of Zacamil, which he always loved.

At the time that he was assassinated, Father Octavio Ortiz Luna had a full schedule. I can describe his final day perfectly. In the morning, he worked with the organizers of the Week of Priestly Identity to make a synthesis of the rich message which he left us that week. In the afternoon, Octavio was the coordinator and I presided at a gathering to give support to the seminary. With a very special gift of grace, he knew how to conduct those meetings so they bore fruit.

From there he left for San Antonio de Abad to celebrate the feast day mass of the day's patron saint. At night he presented the points for reflection for the 30-some youths. Mother Chepita later concretized the spiritual reflection for them with two questions with which they were to begin the day, the day when "The Awakening" was a horrible awakening of death, which gives us this painful message today.

This is the nation that is in reflection here in the cathedral. I want to reflect upon the biblical readings. Forgive me, I am not going to make this very long. I only want to bring into focus what the gospel, theology and pastoral practice say about our reality.

I want to assert that my sermons are not politics. My sermons naturally touch upon politics; they touch upon the reality of the nation so that the gospel can illuminate our condition and tell us what God wants and what he doesn't. The word now shines upon this bloody deed we have heard about (though heard with difficulty, because of a poor sound system). The message for us today can be entitled: an assassination that speaks to us of resurrection.

Let me present three points—there is a new world present; we accept it through conversion; and we must live by faith.

## There is a new world present

Nineveh is the prototype of a frivolous world of human greatness. Nineveh in the first reading (Jonah 3:1-5, 10) represents the great cities: frivolous, egotistic, sinful. And to that frivolous world God sends Jonah, who says, "Within 40 days, if this city does not repent, God will raze it." But today's reading tells us that Nineveh took advantage of the warning. Everyone did penance and God forgave the city.

Christ, the supreme teacher this Sunday, tells us, "The time has come, the reign of God is near." This time that has reached its fulfillment is precisely that of Christ resurrected. He has inaugurated a new era in this world. Happy are those who find that secret of resurrection, because for Christians life on this earth, despite crimes and evil deeds, brings strength and a sign of salvation.

The moment now is pressing, the form of this world passes. God saves in the concrete history of each people and each person. St. Paul says the married should live "as if they were not married, and those who suffer as if they were not suffering: those who rejoice as if they did not have joy, knowing that the form of this world is passing."

Octavio found a treasure; he was sharing it with these youths. This is the great message of Octavio and those who died: the form of this world is passing and the only thing left is the joy of having worked for the reign of God in this world. All the pomp, all the victories, all egotistic capitalism, all the successes in life shall pass away.

What is not passing is love, the conversion into service of money, goods and professional talents and the act of sharing and making all people feel like brothers and sisters. At the end of your life you shall be judged by your love. In this, God has judged Octavio and the deceased youths: in their love.

## We accept this new world through conversion

How lovely it was to see a poor priest who renounced all, living with the simplicity of a field hand and glorying in that title. He knew how to make himself accessible to all who wanted to find in the gospel, characterized by poverty, the great message that God brings in order to save the world: the right use of the goods of the earth by one who is converted, as St. Paul teaches us in the reading today.

The reason for that conversion is that one cannot serve two masters. There is only one God and that God, the true God, asks us to renounce those things that become sinful. The god-money forces us to turn our backs on the God of Christianity. Because people want a god that has his back turned rather than the true God, many criticize the church. They kill Octavio and kill every movement that tries to destroy false idols and give us the true God.

## We must live by faith

That is why, brothers and sisters, Christ tells us, "The reign of God is at hand. Repent and believe in the good news: the faith." The gospel recounts today the first four vocations of the ecclesiastical hierarchy: Peter, and his brother Andrew, and James and his brother John. They leave everything when the Lord invites them so that their conversion might not simply be a cessation from sinning, but fulfilling the will of God.

I want to tell my beloved brother priests—and thank you for being attentive to this message—that the hundred-or-so priests signifying their presence with the priestly stole, around the altar, are the successors of Peter, of Andrew, of James, of John. What God asks of us is precisely what he asked of the four and what he asked of Octavio. And today that tradition presents to us an example with a stole of blood, with a chasuble of suffering, with a disfigured face.

Poor Octavio died with his face crushed. What crushed it? We do not know, but the doctor says, "He died from a crushing blow." The workers at the Auxiliadora funeral home had to put a lot of effort into preparing his body. They could not leave him as he was. Octavio was transformed because he turned the other cheek for Christ. This is what the Lord asks of us.

I rejoice in telling you, beloved Christian brothers and sisters, that today—when it is more dangerous to be a priest—we have more vocations to the priesthood. This year the seminary enrollment is setting a new record. Twenty-seven youths with bachelor degrees are ready to enter a new year of studies at the seminary, because the reign of God in the world enables noble youths to say with the disciple quoted in the gospel, "Let us go with him and die with him."

Each state in life is a vocation. In the second reading, Paul speaks about the concrete situations in which people live: some married, others without matrimonial covenants; some slaves, others lords. Paul says the concrete place in which people live is where God wishes to sanctify them, so that the historical situation will be purified of all sin. All situations in the world are good places to make saints, so long as the persons in them show they are not in agreement with sin. It is the task of Christians to be converted and convert the world from sin to the reign of God, which is already begun.

Each vocation is an instrument of change in a world where sin is enthroned. This community, that has reflected in the light of the word of God, lives in a world where sin is enthroned and is in battle with the reign of God—a battle where neither tanks nor machine guns are necessary, a battle where neither the sword nor the rifle is needed. The battle is fought with guitars and church hymns. Songs are sown in the heart and the world is transformed because "violence, even when it has justifiable motives, is always violence; it is not effective, nor is it dignified," says the pope.

In the presence of these corpses, one feels the natural instinct for vengeance and violence. I pray you may know how to control yourselves and know that there is a power far superior to the power of tanks and also of the guerrillas. It is the power of Christ: "Father, forgive them because they know not what they do." They are ignorant people, pitiable ones! Commitment to Christ's way is far stronger than the violence of artillery. It makes us rise above cruelty to people. This week has been a week in which we have had to cry.

## The week's events

The presence of these bodies reminds us of the kidnapping of Mr. Ernesto Liebes. No one knows where he is; his ill health increases the likelihood of a tragic end. Know how violent kidnapping is. Seizure is not civilized; the disappearances of people are not marks of civilization, nor is jailing people without a trial. All of that is savagery.

I want to say that three kidnapped persons—two Englishmen and a Japanese—are still captive and it is reported they shall not be freed as long as freedom is not given to the five who have disappeared. I pray that the Lord will touch the captors' hearts and that freedom will be given to these our brothers.

This is a week in which we must recall how FAPU occupied the Red Cross, the Mexican embassy and the OAS offices. It also tried to take over Hacienda Chanmico. With these acts the members of FAPU sought publicity and asked for the abolition of the Law of Public Order; they also asked for a general amnesty.

The result of those requests has been that 30 persons have been imprisoned, 86 have been detained, and 19 have been handed over to the courts. The lack of freedom of expression in our land has become evident to many nations of the world. Because of this lack, FAPU feels obliged to use these pressure tactics to which the security corps reacts inflexibly and brutally.

I also want to make it clear that I am unable to do anything in this conflict. Even after the OAS in Washington asked me to intervene, I had to tell them that when I sent a mission of priests, they took away their passports and identification and they were not accepted. Here the church is not recognized as a power that loves human rights.

Our president, in spite of all this, said in Mexico that the church is not persecuted. And he compromises the credibility of our newspapers by having them put this statement in the headlines on the front page. People here in this cathedral know how false this statement is. Our president remarked in Mexico that the crisis in the church was caused by third-world clerics. He denounced

my preaching as being political preaching and said it
does not contain the spirituality that other priests continue to preach. He said I am taking advantage of my
preaching to promote my candidacy for the Nobel Peace
Prize. How vain they think I am!

Concerning the question of whether the "14" are
present in El Salvador, the president denied that there is
anything factual about the story of the "14." He also
denied that there are political prisoners or people who
have disappeared.

Just last night, a journalist from Mexico called me
and asked me what I thought about the remarks. I told
him, "I do not know about them yet." And he read
them to me over the telephone.

I told him, "Well, the best response is that you
should publish in your daily paper what we are living
through here right now: a priest was assassinated by the
National Guard and four other youths died with him."
The reporter expressed interest in these events.

He asked me how I interpret the calumnious and
defamatory campaign against myself and the clergy. I
told him, "That is precisely why we say there is a
persecution against the church: the campaign to create
fear among the Christian communities, is it not persecution? Isn't it also persecution to infringe upon
human rights and those of the nation?" The church
feels that this is her ministry: to defend the image of
God in people.

In conclusion, I told him, "Take note that the conflict is not between the church and the government; it is

between the government and the people. The church is with the people and the people are with the church, thanks be to God!"

## Thoughts that lead us to the altar

Brothers and sisters, through the light of the word of God, these events, these realities of ours, tell us there is only one salvation: Christ our Lord. For that reason the gospel of Mark that leads us to the altar already tells us the reign of God is at hand, the time has been fulfilled, repent and believe.

Lord, today our conversion and our faith are supported by the persons whose bodies are in these coffins. They are the symbols of what our nation is really experiencing, symbols of the noble aspirations of the church that does not want anything other than the salvation of the people.

And look, Lord, this great crowd gathered together in your cathedral is itself a prayer. This crowd is the petition of a nation that weeps, that cries, but does not lose hope because it knows that Christ has not lied. The reign of Christ is close at hand. He only asks us that we be converted and believe in him.

July 22, 1979
# Christ: True Shepherd-King of All People

*Jeremiah 23:1-6*
*Ephesians 2:13-18*
*Mark 6:30-34*

*Archbishop Romero gave this homily following Nicaragua's liberation—the end of her civil war and the overthrow of her oppressive government.*

Beloved brothers and sisters: I believe I interpret the feeling of all of you in making our initial greeting this morning to our sister republic Nicaragua. We greet her with a profound sense of fraternal solidarity and prayer, recognizing that today, more than ever, our countries need spiritual support.

What joy the beginnings of her liberation give us! We pray that this dawning liberty will not be frustrated, but that the Lord, who has been gracious, will continue to be the inspiration of the liberation of the Nicaraguan people. She needs to keep in mind how difficult this moment was to achieve. More than 25,000 dead are not a trifle to be cast aside; Nicaragua must not lay waste her dearly won liberation, a gift from God giving himself in this moment.

Nicaragua's situation evokes two images: the dispersion of the flock and the figure of Christ, the shepherd-king. Nicaragua provides the best background for our meditation on Christ, the shepherd-king, presented in our gospel today. Even though her civil war has ended, its consequences endure; they are great, profound. It can be said of that beloved people what the gospel says today, "I felt sorry for them, I took pity on them, for they seemed to be a people dispersed, like a flock without a shepherd."

Our native land also evokes the image of the dispersed flock. We transpose that figure to ourselves. But as a flock seeks unity and the solution to its problems, so we find in the evangelical message of today's reading God's response to our hopes. The word today offers us the solution: Christ.

I pray that Nicaragua, our own nation and all the nations of the world that find themselves in difficulties, in critical moments, will fix their gaze on the Good Shepherd, the shepherd-king promised through the prophecy of today's first reading and realized in the gospel we read today. We relate our thoughts to the homilies of the last two Sundays on Christ the prophet. Note that each Sunday's reflections help Christians know in a deeper way the central figure whom we follow and love.

We should not forget that the central figure—in whom we, not only as Christians but also as citizens, place our hope, our assurance of salvation—is the Son of God who became human. Jesus Christ under diverse aspects outlines himself in our souls and in our prayers. Pray to Christ, whom we considered as the prophet on previous Sundays, and who today fulfills the role of the great prophet revealing God to us.

We said in the past homilies that the mission of bringing a message has been entrusted to all God's people. Not only the hierarchy (the pope, the bishop, the priests), but also the baptized assembly want to fulfill that mission. We also said that you are a prophetic people, participants in that great prophetic mission of Jesus Christ, the great prophet.

Today we reflect on Christ, the shepherd-king who imparts his power to governments, pastors, people. We look at Christ, shepherd-king of all the nations of the world throughout history. He possesses the key to history, the solution to the critical problems of nations. Only by fixing their gaze on him will the nations find solutions to their crises. If we turn our backs on Christ, we will continue to live meaningless lives, lost like the dispersed flock.

Christ, magnanimous as he is, wants to identify himself with his baptized people of all times, to bring to completion his mission as king. To us, hierarchy and assembly, belongs the task of proclaiming Christ's sole, universal, eternal kingship and making all nations, families, men and women submit to him. It is not a despotic dominion but a dominion of love, the goal of our freedom, as St. Paul says: "Be free to love in Christ Jesus."

In discussing Christ, true shepherd-king of all people, let me treat three topics: the destitution of ill-governed nations, good and bad shepherds of the nations, and Christ as king and shepherd.

## Destitution of ill-governed nations

Today's readings invite us to see the destitution, the misfortune, the misery of nations with bad rulers and bad shepherds. I want to recall that the prophet Jeremiah, in the first reading for today, is speaking to the rulers, the kings of Judah. God called the poor prophet Jeremiah—perhaps the most sensitive prophet, the prophet who by temperament wanted to avoid conflict —to become a prophet of conflict.

Still a youth, he was filled with hope when King Josiah began a national reform, a religious renewal based on God's word. Everything went well until Josiah was killed at Meggiddo. Then the nation suffered calamity: incompetent kings succeeded Josiah; they sought pacts with other countries and made great political mistakes. Jeremiah had to announce some very unappealing news. He had to announce the dispersion, the deportation of the nation, when no one thought the nation could suffer so great a humiliation as being taken captive and led into exile.

Considering how unwelcome this message was, it would have been far easier to turn to flattery and say to the rulers, "All is well; continue!" But the prophet in God's name has to say, "That is not right; it is a mistake," and denounce the sins of his time. Jeremiah saw how his own country was sinking lower and lower. By God's command and in God's words he had to tell Israel's rulers, "Woe to the shepherds who scatter and allow the sheep of my flock to perish."

If we summarize the calamities that befall an ill-governed nation today, we find first that the people are dispersed, just as in the prophecy of today's reading. The authority that should be a moral force to unite, because of its errors is converted into a scattering force. The flock is left without a shepherd.

The second calamity is expulsion, also condemned by Jeremiah: that sin of the rulers who, instead of bringing the sheep into one sheepfold, expel them, repress them, drive them away and do not care for them.

The third calamity is fear and fright which the prophet also denounces: a frightened flock, a terrorized people, an intimidated people. I have lived it—only yesterday, there in the villages of Chalatenango! So much fear one senses in the people! Many people do not come home; they have to stay in the mountains, truly scattered sheep, full of fear.

Fourth and last, the prophet says something about the sheep that get lost. Don't you hear in this the echo of those who have disappeared? The sheep who should have been cared for in the sheepfold by a tender shepherd are persecuted, spirited away, disenfranchised. Jesus takes pity because he sees the multitude like a flock without a shepherd.

The scene the gospel presents clearly depicts Jesus' situation. Christ wants to find a moment's rest, but the people need him, and they go to the desert and find him. The crowd is so great that the gospel cannot describe it with adequate words: "Upon disembarking, Jesus saw a multitude. His heart went out to them because they were like sheep without a shepherd, and he began calmly to teach them." There wasn't any hurry, he wasn't tired anymore. The sheep needed him; he is the Good Shepherd.

But what poor Jesus found was a people who had lost their unity and identity, a people who sought only an earthly solution, ·a political solution for their time. They had forgotten God and there was no one to lead them in their search for him. Jesus begins to teach that the only salvation comes from God, that God loves us, that God has not abandoned us, that we should love one another, that we should not scatter. Such are the teachings of our Lord Jesus Christ.

Even St. Paul in his letter to the Ephesians, in the verse prior to the passage for today, presents us with humanity divided into two groups, Jews and Gentiles. The Jews, precisely because of the privilege of possessing the promise and the revelation, became a nation proud and egotistic. They erected a barrier in the temple so Gentiles could not enter. The Gentiles, non-Jews, were the other part of humanity. The Jews considered them dogs, enemies; and those Gentiles hated the Jews.

Such was the situation. There was no peace, no unity. St. Paul says the Gentiles were "excluded from the citizenship of God, strangers to the covenant and the promise, without hope and without God." How sad: without hope and without God in the world! There is nothing more horrible than a nation that has lost God, has lost its orientation to God. Thus a church incarnated in the world fills me with hope, even though she is criticized.

And I find this echo in you, dearest brothers and sisters who fill this cathedral and the chapels and other places where Christian reflection takes place this morning. Let us reflect on our nation, a nation ill-governed.

Against this background, I want us to note the example Nicaragua gives us today. The price Nicaragua paid for her discontent was more than 25,000 human lives. The nation was not heard. For it to be heard, it felt it had to come to this bloodbath, the result of the absolutization of power. Deified power! A tyrant thinks he is indispensable; it does not matter to him that the whole nation dies.

Nicaragua's experience teaches us that a power cannot keep itself in force with repression nor with corrupt functions. There comes a time when the nation is tired of being exploited and oppressed—a magnificent lesson for those who believe in that power which, in reality, cannot be maintained.

There is something we should keep in mind, which you saw—the published reflection of the United States ambassador. It would be an error, absolutely unpardonable, to close our eyes to the dramatic lesson of the tragic events in our neighboring country. A simple sense of prudence makes us reflect.

Nicaragua provides a lesson for our church. In the Nicaraguan conflict not only the archbishop, but all the bishops in the episcopal conference united themselves and jointly denounced injustice and supported and illuminated the nation. Without identifying itself with the Sandinistas, the church played a very important role because it kept the nation close and faithful. For that reason the Sandinistas now confide in the church. They do not consider her allied with Somoza, nor allied with revolutionary forces. Rather, they consider her the mother church who knew how to understand. At this time of reconstruction, they can count on her for Christian enlightenment.

The dawn of liberation in our brother country, Nicaragua, has awakened great joy, hope and enthusiasm among Salvadoreans. How sad to realize, though, that our government and the ruling classes still do not want to share the joy over Nicaragua's liberation. But that joy befits the church, as does the satisfaction of having been in solidarity with the Nicaraguan church. We feel very close to the Nicaraguan church, and share in its joy and responsibilities—responsibilities ranging from prayer to enlightening people by spreading the gospel.

We are filled with great hope, like someone breathing fresh air, because the guidelines for Nicaragua's new junta say, among other things, that the necessary legislation shall be promulgated to organize an effective democratic government promoting justice and social progress. The judicial branch shall have exclusive jurisdiction; its members must be qualified for their positions and operate independently; this will reestablish the correct application of justice and guarantee citizens the full exercise of their rights.

The absolute guarantee of human rights also fills us with deep satisfaction. It specifies precisely those rights violated while Nicaragua suffered the indigence of an ill-governed nation. For example, on freedom of infor-

mation and dissemination of thought it says: "All the
laws which repress the free transmission and dissemination of thought and freedom of information shall be
abrogated."

On freedom of worship, it states: "The full exercise
of freedom of worship is guaranteed, the free organization of unions, the right to belong to a popular union.
Legislation will be promulgated and actions will be
adopted that guarantee and promote free labor and
trade unions both in the city and countryside." Blessed
be God, that in our Central America there is at least one
place where the rights of people to organize are respected, even if those people be humble field hands.

On personal security, always essential to the fulfillment of human rights, it says: "All repressive laws, especially those that violate the dignity and integrity of
persons, leading to assassinations, disappearances, tortures, illegal seizures and the leveling of homes shall be
abrogated. All repressive institutions, such as the office
of National Security and Military Intelligence Service
—which has served for the political repression of the
nation—and its organizations, shall be abolished." I
might add that these certain organizations are well
known to all.

On the eradication of the vices of the dictatorship, it
states: "The corruption which has been characteristic
of this dictatorship, fraudulent appropriation of
goods, contraband, exemption and illegal dispensation
from taxes, frauds at auctions, deceitful gains from the
sale of property, misuse of state funds, etc., shall be
eradicated."

On rendering justice, it states: "Military and civil personnel involved in crimes against the nation shall be brought before the tribunals of justice."

When the document speaks of the new Nicaraguan army, it says: "In this new national army, corrupt military men and those guilty of crimes against the nation shall not have a place."

Many more statements could be cited, but this one in particular fills me with joy: "A policy of repatriation shall be enacted for the Nicaraguans located in foreign lands, with the objective that they place their knowledge and experiences at the service of the country and participate actively in the work of reconstruction and development."

I hope, sisters and brothers, that our country will not have to undergo a bloodbath to obtain such rights, which are not gifts or favors from the government, but simply the rights of human persons. There is still time for us to regain these rights through rational means. There is still some feeling of goodwill by which the government might become what the Bible speaks of today, "the understanding shepherd of the nation."

I especially want to congratulate our Nicaraguan sisters and brothers who are among us. I distinguish two kinds of Nicaraguan refugees in our country. The first are those who feel happy in this hour in which the liberty of their nation dawns. These I exhort to return home to reconstruct a motherland more just and humane, one that helps make God's kingdom present in our midst.

But there is another group—those who have come fleeing, destroyed by their leader's downfall. To you, also, El Salvador is hospitable. But in welcoming you, I admonish you not to become collaborators to increase or perfect repression in our nation. We will make you feel at home while, like us, you attempt to be converted from injustice, abuse and disorder to that new world exemplified by our shepherd and king, Jesus Christ.

We are glad to tell you that Caritas is fulfilling the mission of being church for the church of Nicaragua. The members of Caritas are sending the following quantities of commodities already procured: nine tons of corn, four tons of beans, a ton and a half of sugar, four tons of rice and some money, which we shall inform you about in more detail later.

The hand of Caritas remains open to receive what you want to give the beloved nation of Nicaragua. I make this plea: may all of us be generous while our sister republic needs our help. There we already see the reflection of our situation. We can say about our nation what the gospel says today: it is "a scattered flock, seeking unity, a passageway out of this blind alley."

The threats continue. The centers of the Salvadorean Council of Juveniles are threatened. We rise in solidarity to issue plaintive calls for help so these threats will cease against some centers where only good is being done. There is a long list of schools, asylums, orientation centers, state centers as well as church centers working in the area of infant and juvenile training; much good work is being done in these centers. I pray the irrational threats will no longer be leveled against this type of institution and other such places that, rather, are in need of assistance from our country.

The teachers who have suffered so many humiliations in the past month began a new phase of their strike this week. They developed a list of petitions, a platform for recovery. Our radio station YSAX made a commentary on it that seems to me to be very accurate. Rather than taking advantage of the strike, it would be better to have recourse to dialogue, which always has a strong importance in our country. ANDES should try everything possible to encourage dialogue. We feel that the strike or the lockout planned for this week, instead of favoring dialogue, might impede it.

It would be advantageous for ANDES to make alliances with diverse educational institutions, especially the Federation of Catholic Schools, which I know to be well disposed to help put pressure on the government to favor its just causes. ANDES has to learn to make alliances with those who work in the field of education, and not pretend to be the only group concerned with the national teaching profession. Other education forces were able to secure substantial favorable gains for the teachers in the last Congress of Educative Reform. Couldn't these other forces, distinct from ANDES but in solidarity with ANDES, fight for their rights through dialogue?

I want to say the same about all those labor disputes still active. I was filled with joy upon seeing in *El Mundo* the story about five labor disputes resolved by the Ministry of Labor. That is precisely the ministry of the Ministry of Labor. The newspaper says about 253

disputes still need reviewing, signing or the granting of
reforms for collective contracts of labor. The whole department of the General Council of Labor is working
on these endeavors.

I want to tell the esteemed workers, with whom the
church has always been in solidarity, that they should
distinguish the field of labor and the factory problem
from other valid areas that many times surpass the
capacity of a joint labor-management meeting. Take
great care, also, lest a strike be politicized and overstep
the limits of labor. In a word: we should know how to
be guided by rationality and not by caprice.

This scattered nation continues lamenting the many
arbitrary seizures and the number of persons who already seem to have disappeared. María Josefina García
and Francisco Martines Canizales were seized in the
canton of Las Ventanas of El Painsnal; María Josefina
later was found assassinated.

Luís Abel Corbera Romero and Antonio Corbera
Romero, brothers, were seized, and it is not known
where they might be. Their father, Esteban, and a four-
year-old daughter, Marcela, were also beaten; they are
already free. Miguel Angel Terezón Ramón, a student,
was captured upon entering his print shop, Offset At-
lántida. On his behalf FAPU has occupied the Church
of El Calvario, demanding his liberty; his family also
asks that the printing equipment be safeguarded. It has
been 23 days since Salvador Flores Benítez was last seen.

David Eleoneo Ponce was captured just outside Pasa-
quina Park; his parents sent me a plea for help. Dis-

turbed and anguished, they write: "On behalf of our son we address you, so you may make a public appeal for the freedom of our son. We want to have him returned to us alive. God grant that he not be dead, as are many who have been seized in our country." I have been a witness to the affliction of this mother; all mothers here can understand what it would be like seeking their son in various detention centers and not being able to find him and not knowing where he might be.

I also know that Dr. Rogelio Monterrosa Sicilia, Santiago de María's attorney, has been threatened with death. I hope that these threats will not increase. Rather, may the voice of conscience be heard, the voice that clearly proclaims the fifth commandment: "You shall not kill."

I want to echo the call for help of the inhabitants of one segment of the suburb named after the tenth of September who have been threatened with relocation for modernization. It would be good to keep in mind that they are a poor people. If the nation's progress is desired it should not be based upon injustices and abuses, above all to the poor.

I want to speak about the fire that occurred at the *La Cronica del Pueblo*. When we left the cathedral last Sunday, someone gave me this note with some money: "In this tragic hour we want to give a hand to the prestigious journalist (Dr. Gonzales) so his valiant newspaper might again be published. We would do the same for the media of the Archdiocesan Office of Communication because it is allied with the suffering people."

I hope this contribution will be imitated. I want to mention some other gestures that display the sympathy that has aided this newspaper. For example, its reporters spontaneously offered to help clean up after the fire, and various workers are increasing their union dues to help with the restoration.

I have talked with the editor-in-chief of the newspaper, Dr. Gonzales, who appreciates these kindnesses. Yes, a lot of goodwilled people are helping him; he wants to continue publishing his paper with the same fairness as before. With the monetary aid he first received, he opened a bank account at the Banco Cuscatlán. Those who want to contribute can send their gift to Banco Cuscatlán account number 05771.

We welcome a new journal, *Agencia Periodistica Independiente, API*. Its 13th issue has already been published. The journal is a fine example of freedom of expression. I congratulate those publishing it and pray that they will always maintain the journal as a voice of truth.

## Good and bad shepherds of the nations

All these thoughts show us that a nation's health depends upon its government, its shepherds. What I am about to say is the second part of my reflection on this homily's theme: Christ, true shepherd of all the nations. What can be extracted from today's readings is that this king-shepherd needs human collaboration. Thus we participate in his dominion by God's law—we Christians and all those still not Christian but who have a responsibility as rulers of the nations, as shepherds of the nations.

Jeremiah speaks to the kings of Judea words that also apply to the church's rulers and shepherds. The responsibility of the civic as well as the religious leader is brought into focus by Jeremiah this morning when he says, "Woe to the shepherds who do not watch over the flock." Since he is referring to the rulers and shepherds of nations and also of the church, together with those of us who participate in that tremendous responsibility, we have to analyze the characteristics of the bad shepherd and the good shepherd.

Jeremiah reprimands the false shepherds by saying: "Woe to the shepherds who scatter my people, the shepherds who shepherd my flock. You scatter my sheep, you disperse them, and do not watch over them. But I shall have you render an account for your evil deeds."

God compels the good shepherd to good governance and inspires the good actions of people that collaborate with him. But God also rigorously observes justice; he threatens to exact an account for every evil action of those fulfilling the sublime role of governing.

When Christ saw the unguided multitude, they seemed to him to be like a great crowd without a shepherd. He said he would exact an account for all evil deeds. It must be terrible to fall into the hands of God when power has been so deified by earthly rules. They have to render account to someone who is above all powers.

In spite of bad shepherds, God takes care of his people, says the first reading. It also says this, which fills us with great consolation: "I myself will gather the remnant of my sheep from all the lands where I have scattered them and I shall bring them back to their pastures so that they will increase and multiply. I shall give them shepherds who will tend them; they will no longer fear nor become frightened, and not one will be lost." This is beautiful!

Everything is not lost; better days are coming; the Lord will rouse us; he will inspire a better sense of direction in our nation so that it will not be a flock without a shepherd, but will truly be governed by love.

## Origin and meaning of authority

I want us to turn our thoughts now to the will of God, coming to us through the Second Vatican Council. It explains how political communities originated and nations came into being:

"Individuals, families and the various groups which make up the civic community are aware of their inability to achieve a truly human life by their own unaided efforts; they see the need for a wider community where each one will make a specific contribution, on an even broader level, to the common good. For this reason they set up various forms of political communities. The political community, then, exists for the common good: this is its full justification and meaning and the source of its basic right to exist.

"The persons who make up the political community are many and varied; quite rightly, then, they may veer toward widely differing points of view. Therefore, lest the political community be ruined while everyone follows their own opinion, an authority is needed to guide the energies of all toward the common good—not mechanically or despotically, but by acting above all as a moral force based on freedom and the sense of responsibility in each person.

"It is clear that the political community and public authority are based on human nature, and therefore belong to an order established by God; nevertheless, the choice of the political regime and the appointment of rulers are left to the free decision of the citizens.

"It follows that the exercise of political authority, either within the political community as such or in representative institutions, must be exercised within the limits of the moral order and directed toward the common good . . . according to the juridical order legitimately established or seen to be established. Citizens, then, are bound in conscience to obey. Accordingly, the responsibility, the dignity and the importance of state rulers are clear.

"When citizens are under the oppression of a public authority which oversteps its competence, they should still not refuse to give or do whatever is demanded of them for the objective common good; but it is legitimate for them to defend their own rights and those of their fellow citizens against the abuse of this authority within the limits of the natural law and the law of the gospel" (*Pastoral Constitution on the Church in the Modern World*, no. 74).

Pardon the quotation, but it tells us what many times is mistakenly understood: "All power comes from God." No one can rule if God does not give them the power. Christ told Pontius Pilate, when Pilate wanted to boast of his power to give life or death, "You would not have any power over me if it had not been given to you from above."

A ruler is the representative of Christ, the shepherd-king, as long as the ruler interprets the thought and the love of that God who gives foundation to all just laws. But when people absolutize their power and set themselves as idols of power and turn against the laws of God, against human rights, and abuse the nation, then we cannot say that their authority comes from God. If they do not act legitimately as God would want, the people, then, for the love of the common good and the objective of being a nation, have to obey only up to a certain point. They always retain the right to their just vindication. The example is very close to home, then, and I pray that we will return to the source of all authority, our Lord.

The gospel today seems to me to include an indispensable point for our reflection. Christ tells his apostles, chosen as shepherds to represent the divine shepherd among people, "Come and rest a while." This rest of Christ has a profound meaning for prayer. To pray —to grow closer to God, to align our authority with God's—is the task of all who govern, be they civil or ecclesiastical. If pastors or rulers separate themselves from God and don't unite their power with God's, then to a greater degree this unifying force, as the council explained, is converted into a scattering force. Then instead of doing good, the ruler does evil.

It is necessary then at this point to call upon all the people of God who from their baptism participate in that prerogative of Christ the king, to ensure that the structures of the earth, the consciences of people, families, society, all that is the world, promote the reign of God. Politics itself should not stray from its true objective; instead, it should be orientated toward God.

Be attentive to Christ, who calls you to frequent reflection so you may know where your responsibility lies and where your life is going. Let us commit our lives to true collaboration with the kingdom of Christ in the world—not contrary to it, separating the kingdom from Christ and handing it over to the reign of sin, to the idols of money and abuse. Instead, may the true God—who has shared his divine power with us, and who will exact an account of our use of it—be content and joyous because some people unite themselves intimately with him, rule according to him and try to direct creation toward him.

## Christ as king and shepherd

In the first reading today, a promise is made, the blessed promise of the Lord, that a just king shall be raised up: "Take heed that the day is coming when I will make a legitimate descendant sprout from David. He shall reign as a prudent king; he shall secure justice and righteousness in the land; in that day he shall save Judah. Israel shall dwell securely and they shall call him the Lord, our justice."

The second reading from St. Paul portrays Christ as the shepherd-king who unites the two divided peoples: "The wall in the temple of Jerusalem which signified the separation of the Gentiles and the Jews has been demolished. He has destroyed it with his own body by dying on the cross."

There hatred was left nailed to the tree, and there the divisions among people likewise came undone. He is our peace. Let us not forget this beautiful phrase from today's reading: "Christ is our peace." He reconciled people with God and gave hatred the deathblow; he came and brought the news of peace, peace for those who are afar, peace for those who are near. Each and every one of us can draw nearer to the Father with one same Spirit.

This is the function of the people of God. I have always wanted us to distinguish between the people of God and people in general. And when I preach all these promises of God, this richness of participation in Christ, prophet, priest and king, I am directing myself to you, the community of baptized people.

Through our baptism, we are responsible for the world: we have to save. As people of God, a prophetic people participating in the royalty of the shepherd-king, all of us baptized Christians have to revise our attitudes so they will not contradict God's reign and his law, but rather will be a faithful collaboration, an image of God's reign in this land.

Christ, I repeat, has a representative here and now— it is us, his church, the community. Looking at the coming week, I reflect on the principal ecclesial task that should be ours as priests, religious and faithful, all pastoral agents. We do not politicize. We illuminate politics with our evangelical light, but our principal duty is to light the lamp of the gospel in our communities.

Thus I am pleased to quote the pope today, as he enlightens the world through words spoken this week to the ministers of agriculture, the experts on nourishment. The pope told more than 150 nations working to help poor farmworkers that they should help them by the redistribution of profits. The pope also said that farmworkers should possess a voice in political decisions. Fabulous words!

I want to tell you all of the pope's message so you may see that while it is true that he encourages priests in their priestly function, he also recommends this other aspect of their ministry, social justice. No one would pay the "kept press" to report this part of the pope's message. It would be nice if the tame media, which publish such interesting articles on the spiritual aspect of priests' ministry, would also be paid to publish the pope's discourses in Oaxaca, Monterrey, and Santo Domingo, and that part of his encyclical where he clearly describes all the abuses that we in the church, including priests, must speak out against.

This week our archdiocesan community fraternally congratulates the dioceses of Santiago de María and Santa Ana who celebrate their patronal feast days—St. James, the apostle, July 25, and St. Anne, July 26.

I have already spoken at length about the feast of Our

Lady of Mount Carmel, but I want to repeat this: We have two great resources in our pastoral work. The first is the presence of Mary in our nation. By God's great blessing, our people are very devoted to Mary. Our second great resource is the richness of our folk religion. Brothers and sisters, let us not lose that inheritance of our parents and grandparents, even if it might seem a bit ridiculous, maybe even a bit imperfect. It is the piety of our people. By cultivating it, we can find the religion that God wants for us at this time.

Yesterday I was in San Miguel de Mercedes rightfully fulfilling my duty of encouraging the Christian communities that are forming there. The Military Reserve Corps stood on both sides of the village entrance to prevent many people from entering the village. The soldiers made me get out of the car and searched it. Even the bishop is suspect! They told me afterward that it was for my security. If it was for my security, I thought, why are they suspicious of my sitting in the car?

I told them, "Why don't you allow these people whom you have detained to enter with me? I am going to enter on foot along with them." They were women, and were not allowed to enter. Afterward I had the opportunity to look for them in San Antonio Los Ranchos. They were waiting for me there because they were very anxious to speak with their pastor.

I believe this situation is similar to the stationing of a retinue of military personnel in the cathedral for our vigil. The officials of our country are trying to undermine the freedom of our church. I would like to request respectfully that these acts not be repeated because they offend our church, even if it is under the pretext of security for the pastor. I want to repeat what I said on another occasion: "The shepherd does not want security as long as the flock does not have security."

Our tour yesterday ended in the nice canton of La Aldeita, where the community of priests, religious and minor seminarians was gathered in a family festival. There I congratulated a newly ordained young deacon, Jaime Paredes. He is already in his new post eager to be of service to us. We hope that he will become a part of that model community and that very soon we might have the joy of ordaining him to the priesthood.

Speaking of the vigil which I already mentioned and omitting the disagreeable subject of military surveillance, I want to congratulate the vicariates that promoted that long pilgrimage of prayer over 40 hours. Many communities of priests and faithful participated, coming from all over the republic. At the vigil I had the opportunity to meet another priest who came to offer his priestly services, Father Luis. He was with us before. I welcome him and wish him great success in our work that so needs his enthusiastic collaboration.

A document has been published and will be featured in *Orientacion* in which the priests reaffirm their desire to fulfill their priestly vocation. In light of reflection on the death of a priest assassinated while carrying out his duties, we priests want to revitalize our lives with prayer, sharing life together, studying and constructing the foundation for God's reign. A statement from the religious women in solidarity with the priests will also be published in the next issue of *Orientacion*.

We congratulate the new board of directors of the Federation of Catholic Schools and Colleges.

I want to announce today that our brother priest, Astor Ruiz, returning from taking a course in Colombia on the Puebla document along with priests and religious women from other nations, was not allowed to disembark at the airport. Instead, he was put on a flight to Guatemala. The same thing happened yesterday to another priest who had labored much among us, Father Juan Deplank. He arrived at the airport and was put on a plane to Guatemala. There surely isn't any freedom for our priests who must cross borders at times in carrying out their mission.

In particular, I want to share the pain of the family of Mrs. Abigail de Girald, who died yesterday in San Miguel.

When we review in this way our thoughts and deeds as a church community, then the interests of the church and the interests of our motherland begin to intertwine. We should not be two enemies with nothing in common. Our church and our country should inspire each other, through the same king and shepherd, Christ, our Lord.

A nation can be a nation only when it is treated with dignity, respected in its rights, and when its rulers and all the people fix their gaze above and wait for him who is our king, our justice, our peace: Christ, our Lord. There is no other solution, dear sisters and brothers. To want to construct a motherland, a future, a better world, while turning our backs on Christ, is like trying to build upon sand.

The winds of violence ruin all positive efforts. Only what is built upon the rock of faith will last—what stands on the inspiration of the king whom God has appointed to rule people in their earthly and heavenly vocation. Governments, bishops, parents, rulers, collaborators, pastoral ministers and all who work for the motherland and for the church can be inspired by Christ, who has compassion for the great crowds and who supports our efforts. Only through him will we find divine resources and find people better than ourselves to help govern the nation.

May the Lord, then, grant that this reflection will lead us to take our place in society wherever our vocation has situated us. Looking toward our Lord, through his inspiration may we know how to give our lives their truest meaning, so each of us may create a motherland and church. So be it.

February 17, 1980
# The Poor: Christ's Instrument of Liberation

*Jeremiah 17:5-8*
*1 Corinthians 15:12, 16-20*
*Luke 6:17, 20-26*

Beloved brothers and sisters: Before delivering my homily, I want to congratulate you because at this moment you are reflecting the true nature of God's people. I am referring to a comment an old Venezuelan politician made to me last Sunday when he was with us. He had come out of curiosity; he was under the impression that our Sunday masses were better defined as political meetings and that people attended out of political curiosity. Were that true, it would alter the character of Sunday mass.

In addition to being a politician, this man is also a great Christian, and he told me, "I have seen that this is truly a Christian assembly because these people sing and pray. Above all, when the time for communion came, I was deeply impressed by the large procession of people that approached the eucharist." I was overjoyed, because what I propose to do is in no way politics.

If by the necessity of the moment I am throwing light

on the politics of my motherland, I do so only as a pastor, shedding the light of the gospel. We must use this light to illumine the ways of the country and to contribute what only the church can give. This is why I am grateful to you that in these gatherings we manifest our identity as God's people.

Furthermore, we are God's people in the midst of the rest of the people, the motherland. We sense our responsibility to meditate upon the gospel so that later each of us in his own situation may be a reproducer of that word, an illuminator of our country's ways.

The historical circumstances are always truly appropriate material for gospel meditation. What circumstances are not appropriate, since the gospel is an incarnation of God in all human situations? At this time when the country is in fear, confusion, insecurity, incertitude, how we hunger for a word of total serenity: the gospel!

Another element—beyond our historical situation—comes into play this Sunday: we find ourselves on the eve of Lent. As God's people, we want to remember our liturgical seasons. Today we have reached the Sixth Sunday in Ordinary Time; the six Sundays between Epiphany and Lent are in Ordinary Time.

Now we interrupt Ordinary Time; next Wednesday we will enter the important seasons of Lent, Easter and Pentecost. When we have finished celebrating the whole Easter season at Pentecost, we shall return to Ordinary Time. Well, now, while we take leave of Ordinary Time and flow into Lent, I think the moment is appropriate to issue a call to God's people. Let us prepare ourselves to begin with all our heart this great spiritual retreat of universal character called Lent.

Next Wednesday, Ash Wednesday, we start Lent. Here, God willing, precisely at 7 p.m. next Wednesday we shall begin Lent. I invite all who can to attend. With the impressive ceremony of the ashes which signify both our mortality and our immortality, we enter into serious reflection.

There is no better time than Lent, I believe, to help our motherland, if we live the season as a great campaign of prayer and penance. We are not politicians who confide in mere human strength. We are, above all, Christians, and we know that if the Lord does not build our civilization, the builders build in vain. That is why we know that our strength comes from prayer and conversion to God.

This long pilgrimage we begin Wednesday will take us to Easter and Pentecost, Lent's two great goals. People do not mortify themselves because of a neurotic desire for suffering. God has not created us for suffering. We fast, do penance and pray because we have a positive goal that we reach through conquering self: Passover, resurrection.

We do not celebrate merely a Christ who rose without us. During Lent we are empowered to rise with him to a new life—to become precisely those new people needed today in our country. We should not just seek changes in structures because new structures are worth nothing when there are no new people to manage them and live in them.

Turning to Pentecost, the coming of the Holy Spirit, let us prepare ourselves so that our hearts will be like clean vessels, well disposed so the Spirit of God may come with all the strength of sanctity to transform the face of earth. This is what is lacking in our motherland: a greater awareness of God's Spirit, a greater sense of resurrection, a deeper renewal of life.

Lent invites us to look inside ourselves and be renewed. I believe today's readings do precisely that: they call us to interior renewal. They form a precious prologue to Lent, and relate to a statement in the Puebla document on why we should be filled with hope: "Poverty in Latin America is tangible. Its seal marks the immense majority, who not only are open to the beatitudes and the preference of the Father, but also to the possibility of being the true protagonists of their own development" (1129).

The poor are a sign in Latin America. The majority of our countries are poor; thus they can receive God's gifts and, filled with God, they can transform their societies. I am pleased that, alongside the poor, Puebla also applies this sign value to young people. Beloved youngsters, you are like the poor in Latin America, the signs of God's presence.

The poor and the young constitute the rich hope of the church in Latin America; their evangelization has precedence. Our church feels a special love and responsibility for the majority—the poor and the young. They are going to reconstruct our motherland.

Let us be truly confident this will really happen if everyone adopts the disposition of poor people and young people, who already constitute the vast majority of our country. May the risen Lord find in these two great signs of El Salvador, the poor and the young, the best instruments for reconstruction. Let us not lose hope, because El Salvador has many poor people and young people, themselves the source of hope.

That is why I am taking the theme for today's homily from a section on poverty in the Medellin documents. They see poverty denounced by God, they call it a spirit and a commitment. The theme of this homily is poverty in the beatitudes, the strength of the true liberation of the people. The three points I will cover are those Medellin lists as the strength of liberation: poverty is denounced by God; poverty is a spirit; poverty is a commitment.

My treatment of these points will, if God wills it, give us a clear idea of what we so often repeat: that the church has made a preferential option for the poor, and that the church can only be a true church if it is converted and commits itself to poor and suffering people.

## Poverty is denounced by God

First of all, Medellin asks (and I am going to reinforce this thinking with the liturgical texts for today), why is poverty denounced by God? The Medellin text says, "Poverty, taken as a lack of the goods of this world, is in itself evil. The prophets denounce it as contrary to the will of the Lord, and most of the time as the fruit of the injustice and sin of people" (14,4).

What does Jesus do in this gospel of the beatitudes? First, the gospel says Jesus "comes down."

How delightful it is to reflect with Jesus who lowers himself, says the gospel. Various expressions in the gospels reveal profound ways of seeing Jesus. We see him descending from the mountain, descending from the heights to intermingle on the plain with common people. Having descended he begins to preach the word to them, and thus today's gospel begins: "Blessed are you poor, for the kingdom of God is yours."

There are poor people, people that hunger or that weep, because there are rich people. In the conclusion to these four beatitudes, Christ denounces those responsible for poverty, hunger and suffering. Why do the blessed who suffer, cry and hunger experience such evil? The gospel is powerful today when it points out the causes of these needs:

"Woe to you rich, because you have your consolation now! Woe to you who are satisfied, because you shall hunger! Woe to you who laugh now, because you shall suffer and cry!" The message of all the Old Testament prophets resounds in Christ's voice. How thunderous are the prophets when they cry out against the way people pile house upon house, land upon land, and make themselves masters over the whole country!

The existence, then, of poverty as a lack of necessities is denounced. Brothers and sisters, those who say that

the bishop, the church, the priests have caused the disorder in our country want to gloss over the reality.
Those who have done the greatest damage are the ones
who caused the horrible social injustices our people
endure. Therefore the poor have marked out the way
the church should go. A church that does not unite
itself to the poor in order to denounce from the place of
poor the injustices committed against them is not truly
the church of Jesus Christ.

I want to take this opportunity to tell you this was
precisely the theme of my address at the University of
Louvain in Belgium where they asked me to speak on
politics and faith. That is the general theme for all the
conferences of that celebrated university this year.

I chose to enflesh that concept with the political dimension of faith stemming from the poor. And I tried
to show how in El Salvador the key for understanding
the Christian faith is the poor. They delineate our archdiocese's ministry. At Louvain I said our Salvadorean
world is not an abstraction: it is a world mostly made
up of poor and oppressed men and women. In this
world, the poor are the key to understanding the Christian faith, the political dimension of that faith, and the
church's action.

The poor tell us what the world is and what service
the church can offer the world. The poor tell us what
the *polis*—the city—is, and what it means for the
church to live in the world, in the city. Allow me, I told
my audience at Louvain, to explain briefly the situation of the poor of my nation, whom I want to repre-

sent, and the participation of our church in the world
in which we live. And I began to narrate the adventure
of our church here in El Salvador. I posed the question,
what are we doing?

In the first place, we are incarnated in the poor; we
want a church that is shoulder to shoulder with the
poor people of El Salvador. Every time we come closer
to the poor, we discover the true face of the suffering
servant of Yahweh. There we come closer to knowing
the mystery of Christ who becomes human and becomes poor through us.

What else does the church do here? I told the audience that we proclaim the good news to the poor, but
not demogogically to exclude everybody else. On the
contrary. Those who have listened in only a secular
way to the news and have not led lives of faith are now
hearing through the church the words of Jesus: "The
reign of God is at hand! It is ours. Happy are you, the
poor, because yours is the reign of God!" And from
there we also have good news to proclaim to the rich:
become poor in order to partake of the goods of the
kingdom of God, which belong to the poor.

The church in El Salvador also has another role, I
told the people at Louvain: it is committed to defending the poor. The poor of our country hear from the
church the voice of Israel's prophets denouncing those
who use violence and pile up booty in their palaces,
those who trample upon the poor, those who make the
reign of violence come closer as they lie upon their
marble beds, those who join house to house and annex

lands to lands in order to occupy the whole locale and become the only people in the country. These texts from the prophets are not distant voices which we read reverently in our liturgy. They represent the realities of everyday life; we live such cruelty and intensity each day.

And that is why, I tell you, the church suffers the same destiny as the poor: persecution. Our church glories in having mixed the blood of priests, catechists and communities with the blood of other people who have been massacred. The church has always carried the mark of persecution. Precisely because it hinders the unjust, it is slandered. The cruel do not want to hear from her the voice that cries out against injustice.

The second part of my discourse at Louvain was about how the church is enriched in this work for the nation, for the poor. This work gives the church a clearer sense of sin, because the poor themselves denounce sin. In coming closer to the poor, the church better understands that sin is a grave matter. Sin brought death to the Son of God and sin continues to bring death to the children of God.

That fundamental truth of faith is seen daily in situations in our country. One cannot offend God without offending one's brothers and sisters. It is not just for effect that we repeat once more that structures of sin exist in our country. Certain structures are sinful because they produce the fruits of sin, the death of Salvadoreans—the rapid death caused by repression or the slow death of institutional oppression. For that reason we have denounced the sin of injustice.

This mystery of poverty helps us understand more clearly the redemption of Jesus Christ, who became like us in everything except sin to redeem us from our sins and make us better understand who God is. God wants to give us life. Every person who takes life or damages life by mutilating, torturing and repressing is showing us the contrast between their actions and the divine image of the God of life, who respects the freedom of people.

This is the first thought in today's homily. I rejoice that I presented these considerations in a country as developed as Belgium, and could convey to some degree what my listeners there found it difficult to comprehend. Namely, I described a church that does not become involved in politics but rather, by speaking the prophetic word of God through the poor, denounces the country's injustice.

Furthermore, poverty is holy because it cries out to denounce our church itself. This is a message from the Puebla document: "The commitment to the poor and oppressed and the emergence of basic communities have helped the church discover the evangelizing potential of the poor, inasmuch as they constantly question her, call her to conversion, and inasmuch as they also realize in their lives the gospel values of solidarity, service, simplicity and availability to accept God's gift" (1147).

Critics should always be ready in turn for criticism. If the church denounces injustices, she should also be willing to listen to criticism and be ready to convert. The poor are a constant cry that denounces not only

social injustice but also the lack of generosity in our
own church.

## Poverty is a spirit

And so, first of all, poverty is something denounced.
The second thing I want to say today is that poverty is a
spirit. And I am interested in what the documents of
Medellin have to say about this: "Spiritual poverty is
the theme of the poor of Yahweh. Spiritual poverty is
the attitude of openness to God, the disposition of those
who have all their hope in the Lord. Even though they
value the goods of this world, they do not cling to them,
but recognize the superior value of the good of the
kingdom" (14,4).

Poverty is a spirituality, an attitude of the Christian;
it is a disposition of the soul open to God. That is why
Puebla says that the poor are the hope of Latin America,
because they are better disposed to receive God's gifts.
That is why Christ says with so much emotion:
"Happy are you, the poor, because yours is the kingdom of God!" You are better able to understand this
than those who kneel in front of false idols and trust in
them. You do not have these idols; you do not trust
them because you have no money or power, but are the
most helpless and poorest of all.

You are heir to the kingdom of God, insofar as you
live that spirituality in truth. The poverty which Jesus
Christ dignifies is not mere material poverty, not the
state of having nothing—that is evil. Rather, the poverty of the beatitudes is a conscious poverty. It is a

poverty that does not passively accept the cross and sacrifice because it knows that is not God's will.

The poor find that to the extent that poverty becomes a consciousness, a spirituality, a gift, a disposition of openness to the Lord, it becomes holy. As a result of this holiness, they will discover poverty to be the
best liberator of their own people. The church is forg-
ing these liberators of the nation. You Christians, in
the measure in which your poverty is converted into
spirituality, in that same measure you also are liberators of our nation.

Let us note the point at which Christ speaks that
beatitude so that we might see its far-reaching effect.
Let us not separate it from the context of Israel's history. How was Israel born? Of the promise of God to
Abraham, an old man, sterile, without children, a man
with a barren wife. God tells Abraham, "From your
descendants I am going to make a large nation." Israel
begins through a sign of poverty, an almost absolute
limitation: Abraham and Sarah cannot have children
and yet God tells them that he is going to give them a
nation of descendants. Abraham accepts this through
faith and that nation becomes a reality. And that nation
finds a promise in God: I am going to give you a land.
By means of a guide, Moses, God takes them to that
promised land. In that promised land God offers them
the law, his covenant.

But that nation is not faithful. Because of infidelity
Israel goes into exile and there nostalgically laments
the loss of the land God gave it and took away because

of sin. Israel bears the sign of poverty. "Now," God tells Israel, "repent." The prophets call Israel to repentance and it does receive God's forgiveness. And the nation returns from Babylon and rejoices that it is once more in its own country.

However, back in that country Israel suffers many political vicissitudes! The one that interests us now is this: one day the Roman empire took possession of that land and the Roman army took over its administration. An occupied nation! In that nation dominated by Rome, Christ makes his appearance. To that nation, politically subjected to a foreign imperialist power, Christ preaches, "Blessed are you poor, because yours is the reign of God!"

I recall this context so the gospel beatitudes will not mystify us. St. Matthew, in a phrase hard to understand, tells us, "Blessed are the poor in spirit." Many have twisted that phrase to the point of saying that all are poor, even the oppressor. That's not true in the context of the gospel. Luke simply says the "poor" are the ones in need, the ones suffering oppression, the ones who need God to remedy that situation.

But Jesus Christ does not come with weapons; he does not promote revolutionary political movements, although by his doctrine all the revolutions on earth become part of the great liberation from sin unto life eternal. He gives goals for those fighting to liberate nations. When Christ speaks of "the poor in spirit," he is referring to the Israelites incarnate in a specific nation. It's another way of saying to them: you have to be

free also, you have to someday shake off the yoke of
those who have invaded this land, but you have to do it
with the spirituality of the poor.

The virgin Mary, the most spiritual person Yahweh
made, understood it this way. When she sings in her
Magnificat that God frees the humble and the poor, the
political dimension resounds. She says, "God sends the
rich away empty and fills the poor with goods." Mary
even speaks words we today would call insurrectionary:
"He casts down the mighty from their thrones when
they become an obstacle to the tranquillity of the nation!"

This is the political dimension of our faith; Mary
lived it, Jesus lived it. He was an authentic patriot of a
people under the domination of a foreigner, and beyond doubt he dreamt they would be free. But, mean-
while, he had to pay tribute to Caesar: "Render to Caesar what is Caesar's, but don't give to Caesar what belongs to God. Give to God the things that are God's!"

This spirituality explicitly characterizes today's first
reading. Without a doubt Christ, when he spoke,
echoed the old prophets. Thus the church today gives
us a gospel text in which Christ quotes from the Old
Testament. Close to the theme of the beatitudes of the
poor, of the ones who hunger, of those who suffer, of
those who weep, comes the cry of Jeremiah: "Cursed be
the ones who put their trust in people. In flesh they seek
their strength, straying in their heart from the Lord.
They shall be like the thistle in the steppe, they shall

not see good; they shall inhabit the aridity of the desert,
a land that is salty and inhospitable.''

Jeremiah envisions aridity for the persons who have
put their trust in the things of the earth. That is why he
says, "Woe to you rich! If now you seem like flourish-
ing trees, tomorrow you shall be dried up like the
steppe in the aridity of your own egotism." The prophets describe the contrast: blessed are those who put
their trust in the Lord!

Don't you hear the echo of Christ's words: "Blessed
the poor, those who trust in the Lord and place their
trust in him"? The poor person shall be like a tree planted
by water; near running water it extends its roots. When
summer comes, it shall not feel the heat and its leaves
shall remain green. In the year of drought it does not
weaken, it does not cease to bear fruit. These are the true
poor, whose spirituality is great faith in the Lord. The
curse of the rich is to separate themselves from the Lord
and place their trust in the flesh, in other words, in the
valued things of the world.

That is why, sisters and brothers, it is not a mark of
prestige for the church to be in good standing with the
powerful. What gives the church prestige is to know the
poor sense the church as their own, to know the church
has a mission in the world to call all—even the rich—to
repent and be saved as part of the world of the poor,
who alone are the blessed.

The idea of poverty as a spirit fits in with today's
second reading, which gives us a basis for our hope. St.
Paul writes to the Christians at Corinth where errone-

ous ideas about the resurrection were current. Some said, "There is no resurrection!" They laughed at Paul when he spoke about the resurrection, but Paul held to his faith. He wrote about the witnesses to Christ's resurrection: "He was seen by more than 500 disciples . . . and last of all he appeared to me, the one who is relating this. I persecuted the church and did not believe in the teachings of the church, but I have seen him and have been converted and am now preaching him."

St. Paul is a marvelous witness to the resurrection because, if there was any man who had not wanted to believe in Jesus or in the resurrection, it was the persecutor Saul. He believed Christians were deceiving his Jewish companions; that was why he persecuted them. And to this Paul, convinced that Christ did not live, Christ appeared—living. Now that he had given his life over to that great truth, he tells the Corinthians their error, "Christ has risen! . . . And if you say that the dead do not rise, why is it that I have seen Christ resurrected?"

## Poverty is a commitment

As my third point today, I want to present this idea: poverty is a force for liberation. Besides being a sinful reality to be denounced, and besides being a Christian spiritual force, poverty is a commitment.

The word "Christian" reminds me I have to give the example of being Christian. All you beloved brother priests, religious women and all you baptized who call yourselves Christian, hear what Medellín says: "Poverty as a commitment, through which one assumes voluntarily and lovingly the conditions of the needy of this world in order to bear witness to the evil which it represents and to spiritual liberty in the face of material goods, follows the example of Christ who took to himself all the consequences of humanity's sinful condition and who being rich became poor in order to redeem us."

This is the commitment of the Christian: to follow Christ in his incarnation. If Christ, who was the God of majesty, became a humble person, lived with the poor, and finally gave his life as a slave on the cross, we should do the same, through our Christian faith. A Christian who does not wish to live this commitment of solidarity with the poor is not worthy of the name Christian.

Christ invites us not to fear persecution. Believe this, brothers and sisters: those who commit themselves to the poor have to be open to the same destiny as the poor. And in El Salvador we already know the destiny of the poor: to disappear, to be captured, to be tortured, to reappear as corpses.

Whoever wants the privileges of this world and not the persecutions of commitment to the poor should hear the tremendous antithesis in the gospel today: "Blessed are you when people hate you, exclude you, insult you, and cast your name out as evil because of the Son of Man. Rejoice on that day and leap with joy because your reward will be great in heaven."

With immense joy and gratitude I want to congratulate the priests. More than ever they are committed to the poor; more than ever they are defamed. Precisely because they are committed to alleviating the misery of our nation, they are insulted. I want to rejoice with the religious men and women committed to this nation unto the point of heroism in suffering with it. They remain at their tasks with the Christian communities and catechists while cowards flee.

Those who want to escape the consequences of persecution, of slander, of humiliation, should hear what Christ has said this Sunday: "Woe to you when everyone speaks well of you; that is what your ancestors did with the false prophets!" How sad is the praise of the world! If Christians who suffer slander and persecution wanted to live well, they could very easily betray their Christianity and worship money as do people who live well in this world, but woe to you who do that.

Today's second reading also confirms this truth about poverty as commitment. The extreme manifestations of poverty are sin and death. No one is more miserable than people in sin, and no one is poorer than a corpse. And these are the ones to whom Christ committed himself: the sinners and the dead. Christ's redemption liberates a crippled world.

People are not fulfilled until they are able to free from sin those who are sinners, and from death those who are dead; this is what the great liberator offers. Blessed are those who work for the political liberation of the world, keeping in mind the redemption wrought by him who saves from sin and saves from death.

The second reading for today encourages people who fight for the world's resurrection. Believe in the resurrection. Do not doubt that Christ has risen and that he has saved us, through his cross and glory, from sin and death. We all die, but the one who believes in Christ will live forever. In the heavens we shall sing the victory of immortality; the struggles to liberate the earth will seem mere skirmishes. The great liberation is Christ's.

Those who incorporate Christian faith in the freedom fight of their people have the guarantee of an integral liberation, complete and immortal. Those who want to separate themselves from the Christian liberation and fight only for temporal things—better wages, cheaper commodities, drawing more people into political activity, establishing new structures that tomorrow will be old—those people make only temporal, transitory improvements. The only enduring element in that type of work is to have labored in a Christian spirit.

You who live in organized groups or form political parties, do not forget, if you are Christian, to live your Christian commitment to the poor profoundly, intensely. Many people already do that, thanks be to God, because many helping the poor came from our ecclesial communities. The sad thing is that many others lost their faith and cut themselves off from the most important aspect of life.

Many Christians, however, continue fighting in the popular political organizations without betraying their faith. They turn to their Christian communities to let the faith nurture their political struggle and to let the faith confront their political objectives. They are on the right path. I tried to make that point in my fourth pastoral letter: today one of the more urgent pastoral works in the archdiocese is the ministry of "accompanying." In other words, we should work alongside youths to help them mature in their faith. We must stand beside the men and women who belong to political groups so they can live the political commitment of their faith, without betraying their faith. Faith has a political dimension, but it is always faith in the Lord's eternal resurrection which rescues people from sin.

I pray the church will not be despised when it calls out from this perspective against the imperfections, abuses, strategies or limitations of political groups. Don't misunderstand her. Listen to her as a mother and listen to her as a teacher of the faith if you truly want to honor your calling as a Christian. Truly live the faith; it is useless to be a Christian in name only.

We are filled with zeal to make our church resemble the ideal Christ presents to us today: a church of the poor. We do not mean a church limited to a particular social class; we simply recognize that Christ saves all who want to be saved by means of the poor. Let us try, brothers and sisters, to make our archdiocese such a church. I hope my words on various events in our archdiocese will further that intention.

The first event for our consideration is Lent. I already announced it is beginning, but I repeat the announce-

ment and invite everyone to come here Wednesday at 7
p.m. to solemnly inaugurate Lent.

Many will hear on the radio what Father Fabian
Amaya announced on Friday. Namely, it is authorized,
in the communities that do not have priests, for someone to receive ashes at the parish mass and then take the
blessed ashes back to the communities. There, the one
in charge of the community—a lay man, a sister or a lay
woman—should have a service to distribute ashes,
which primarily consists of an invitation to conversion. We shall have the order of the service copied at the
chancery. All who want to can go there and get the leaflet detailing what can be done.

If you cannot get that leaflet, read some passage from
the Bible, explain the significance of the imposition of
ashes, reflect on the meaning of Lent, and draw near
with humility to receive the ashes with the words of
Christ. He tells us the reign of God is at hand; be converted to the gospel.

No one should be left without ashes. If you cannot
attend the community ceremony, conduct the service at
home. The father, as the true priest of the family, can
take some ashes and celebrate with his family the beginning of Lent and impose ashes at home. The holy ashes
are not part of a sacrament but simply part of a rite to
remind us that we are dust and to dust we shall return.
What is important is that each person be converted to
the Lord. We want this beautiful rite to reach all the
homes. We ask everyone to collaborate so the beginning of Lent will be widely observed and our whole

archdiocese will enter into a season of conversion, prayer, fasting and penance.

To fast means to eat only one principal meal. Those who by custom eat their principal meal at lunchtime should eat a little for breakfast and supper, so the stomach suffers a little. Those who by custom make supper the main meal should eat a little for breakfast and lunch and then take their nourishment at supper. But the official fasts are only two: Ash Wednesday and Good Friday.

Abstinence, which means not eating meat, is obligatory on Fridays during Lent for those who have already completed their 14th birthday and have not reached the age of 60. "What does eating or not eating meat add?" one might ask. Well, it adds nothing! What it means is a control of the will, a sign to God you are depriving yourself because of your excesses, your abuses of liberty. This is the meaning of penance.

Let us go beyond these legal, official observances and live a Lent where we do not emphasize eating so much meat. More importantly, let us mortify ourselves and share with those who have less than the little we have. Live that sharing, love and charity. Above all make a great effort at reconciliation with enemies in this Lenten season. Know how to forgive, know how to rise in love with Christ in the coming Passover.

The document in which I make my Lenten appeal will appear in *Orientacion* this coming week. Today I proclaim to you the "reward" of Lent: Passover, which will be Holy Saturday, April 5, and Sunday, April 6.

That vigil night should be the most solemn of our liturgical year. Prepare yourselves. Above all, prepare the
young people to celebrate an Easter in which Christ is
truly expressed as living and increasing the hope in the
world through the youth.

The other "reward" of Lent comes 50 days after the
resurrection, Pentecost, the coming of the Holy Spirit.
We want to celebrate Pentecost with solemn celebrations of confirmation throughout the diocese. I already
know several parishes are preparing youths for confirmation. Young people, most of all, prepare yourselves
well so that on the day of Pentecost you will be apostles
receiving the Holy Spirit whom Christ secured for us
with his death in order to revive the holiness, the hope
of this world.

Confirmation is so rich a sacrament; it is especially
appropriate at Pentecost. I hope we will truly make our
feast of Pentecost this year an authentic renewal of the
face of our diocese. I urge our beloved pastors, the religious women and catechists to help us to prepare the
youth who have not yet been confirmed, so that they
might be a sign of the presence of God's Spirit on Pentecost, May 25.

Let me continue with other news. The Sisters of
Charity are celebrating the virgin's apparition to St.
Catherine Labouré 150 years ago. The sisters of Casa
San Vincente of Santa Tecla invite you to their home
where they will have a beautiful program commemo-
rating this feast.

I celebrated the feast of Our Lady of Lourdes in the

parish dedicated to her at Colon. One of the customs
there is for the children to give a special sign of peace. A
stream of children approach the altar to greet the priest
and give him the sign of peace. I truly felt the children
were little angels of earth who bring peace, which our
country so badly needs.

Another custom for which I congratulate the parish
is the invitation that Mr. Hilario issues (I forget his last
name) to pray the rosary. Although he sits in a wheel-
chair, he is a very active man, and is always asking
everyone into his home to pray the rosary.

In the canton of San Rafael, Candelaria, Cuscatlán,
the statue of the patron, the Archangel Raphael, was
enthroned yesterday afternoon.

In Guazapa a new group of Carmelite Daughters of
the Church was formed. The objective of this group of
women is to share the life of the people, becoming an
incarnation in the village without belonging to a religious congregation. They are going to awaken many
vocations, as is already happening among the youth.
Young people truly want to consecrate themselves to
God. But some of them have no way to express that
desire. May the Holy Spirit illuminate us, and may
many young women truly want to live the holiness of
the evangelical counsels which we are living today.

The church building in Guazapa is being enlarged.
The parishioners hope that in Guazapa and in the different cantons, people will collaborate with the committee trying to give this sign to the people: a church
building where the community can come together.

Tonight we shall hand over the administration of Colonia Santa Lucia in Ilopango to the new pastor, Father Luís Recinos. This young priest came from Nicaragua to continue his studies and volunteered his service in ministry, which we deeply appreciate.

An emergency committee has been formed for the Archdiocese of San Salvador. United with the Ecumenical Committee for Humanitarian and Charitable Aid, this emergency committee hopes to answer the many needs of the diocese.

When I entered church I was handed a note which asked if forming this committee signified a possible civil war. I tell you we are not trying to alarm anyone. We are not preparing for civil war. However, a tremor of fear comes over us unexpectedly. Isn't this a civil war in which we are living, in which people kill one another?

Do not fear, this is not an alarm. War might break out, but that is not why we have organized our committee. Rather it was formed precisely because we had to worry about lodging people in church buildings after the massacre of January 22. The church always has to be hospitable in meeting people's needs.

One is moved to pity here at the cathedral. Some consider a church building to be only for worship. Lately, though, the cathedral has been filled with people who have come fleeing from those cantons where they cannot return because they are persecuted. If they could not find refuge in the church building, they would have to hide in the hills. This makes us realize the church always has to live prepared for emergency.

I want to thank you—forgive me for not having done so earlier—for the many congratulatory notes sent me following the honor that was given to our diocese at the University of Louvain. It was a special honor to receive a telegram from one of the members of the government junta, Dr. Avalos, whom I cordially thank for manifesting solidarity with us. The telegram reads: "I give you my sincerest congratulations on your high honors at the Catholic University of Louvain, Belgium. I want to take this opportunity to renew the demonstration of my highest consideration and regard for you. Dr. José Ramón Avalos Navarette."

Also in a very special way, I want to thank the National Commission on Human Rights, the M.N.R. Party and the Office of Salvadorean Workers. They have publicly manifested their solidarity with us on this occasion. And I thank all the persons who have expressed this same sentiment or have prayed for me. May God reward you.

## Comments on civil events

From within this church that must be a light to the world, we look toward the world around us to try to illuminate it with faith. When I spoke at Louvain about the political dimensions of faith, I concluded by saying that the world of the poor marks out for our church the limits of the political dimension of faith. In our diverse political climate our concern is for the poor.

I didn't want to detail all the ins and outs of politics in my country. I preferred to explain at Louvain the profound roots of the church in this explosive world of El Salvadorean socio-political matters. I tried to make clear the ultimate criterion (one with both a theological and historical basis) for the involvement of the church in this field: the needs of the poor.

To the extent the poor are affected by various political projects, the church will continue to support the projects precisely in its role of being church. That is the way the church sees its responsibility at the moment of this homily: to support what will benefit the poor, as well as denounce what might be bad for the people. With this criterion, we are going to speak out about some of this week's events.

For example, Decree 114 has been promulgated, prompting much discussion and controversy. The church is not interested in legal statements that many times hide selfish motives. What interests the church is whether or not that decree will truly be a step toward the transformation the poor need. If the decree means something good for the poor, the church is in agreement with it; if it does not signify anything for the poor, then the decree does not capture the church's interest.

Lamentably, the government's promises are still not concretized into deeds. What has become more evident this week is that neither the junta nor the Christian Democrats (the leading party) are governing the country. They are only "volunteering" to pretend to govern, so that at the national and international levels they make it appear so.

The February 12 massacre of the protesters from MERS and the bloody removal of the occupants of the Christian Democratic headquarters clearly show they are not the ones who govern. Instead, the most repressive sector of the armed forces and security corps rules this nation. The directors of the Christian Democrats recognized these acts can only be considered acts of disobedience. They violate the agreement the junta made through Colonel Majano when the junta was assured there would be no intervention from the security corps.

It did not matter to the members of the security corps that the daughter of one of the junta members and the wife of the minister of education were there when the violence occurred. Little did they care for the lives of the occupants. They killed many of them. Horrible descriptions have been given by eyewitnesses.

If the junta and the Christian Democrats don't want to be accomplices to so much abuse of power and so many crimes, they should identify and condemn those responsible. It is not sufficient for them to say they are going to investigate. There are eyewitnesses worthy of credibility; the junta members and the party should be able to shorten the investigations. Also, the families of those assassinated should receive compensation from the security corps.

The hopes that they will penalize those responsible for the repression of previous regimes are quickly fading. The actual military authorities and those of the security corps, like their predecessors, continue to stain their hands with blood. They repress the people now more than before.

Along with this, it has become evident that the government lacks popular support; its sole foundation is the armed forces and the aid of some foreign powers. This reveals the grave situation of the Christian Democrats: their presence in the government along with other private political and economic interests are moving countries such as Venezuela and the United States to support an alternative that claims to be anti-oligarchical but in truth is anti-people.

## Letter to President Carter

Moved by this disturbing fact (that the government represses the people), I have dared to write the following letter to President Carter. I will send it after you have given me your opinion of it.

*Mr. President:*

*In these past few days a bit of news appeared in the national press which has disturbed me very much. According to the story, your government is studying the possibility of supporting the junta of our government with military and economic aid.*

*Because you are a Christian and have demonstrated you want to defend the rights of all humans, I want to explain how I, as pastor, see this news and to give you a concrete recommendation.*

*The information that the United States government*

*is studying the way in which to build up the armaments of El Salvador greatly disturbs me. Reportedly, you plan to send military equipment and consultants to train three Salvadorean battalions in logistics, communication and intelligence. If in fact this information is correct, the contribution of your government will do nothing to support greater justice and peace in El Salvador. Without doubt, it will intensify injustice and the represssion of the organized people who so many times have fought for their fundamental human rights.*

*Unfortunately, the junta and above all the armed forces and the security corps have not shown their capacity to resolve, through practical and institutional politics, our grave national problems. Generally they have simply turned to repressive violence, producing a number of dead and wounded much greater than those of the previous military regimes whose systematic violation of human rights was denounced by the Interamerican Commission on Human Rights itself.*

*The brutal manner of their actions was exemplified when the security corps recently evacuated and assassinated the occupants of the Christian Democratic headquarters in spite of the fact that neither the junta nor the party, it seems, authorized the operation. This is evidence that the junta and the Christian Democrats do not govern the country. Rather, political power is in the hands of unscrupulous military men who only know how to repress the people and favor the interests of the Salvadorean oligarchy.*

*If it is true that last November "a group of six Americans was in El Salvador distributing $200,000 worth of* gas masks and bulletproof vests and giving instructions on the use of these against demonstrators," you yourself must know that from that moment the security corps, with greater personal protection and efficiency, has repressed the people even more violently by using deadly weapons.

As a Salvadorean and as the archbishop of the Archdiocese of San Salvador, I have the obligation to see to it that faith and justice reign in my country. Therefore, if you truly want to defend human rights, I ask you:

—to prohibit the sending of military aid to the Salvadorean government;

—to guarantee that your government will not intervene directly or indirectly with military, economic, diplomatic, etc., pressures to try to determine the destiny of the Salvadorean nation.

At this time we are living through a grave economic-political crisis in our country. However, without question, moment by moment our nation is being conscienticized and organized. Through this process, our people have begun to make themselves capable of managing and taking responsibility for El Salvador's future. They are the only ones capable of overcoming this crisis.

It would be a deplorable injustice if, through the introduction of foreign weapons and force, the development of the Salvadorean nation was frustrated. Foreign intervention would suppress and impede the autonomous decision-making process that our country *should follow, a process already begun along appropriate economic and political lines.*

*It would be a violation of a right which the Latin American bishops recognized publicly while in Puebla when we called for "the legitimate self-determination of our nations: that they be allowed to organize themselves according to their own genius and historicity and to cooperate in a new international order" (Puebla 505).*

*I hope that your religious feelings and your sensitivity to the defense of human rights will move you to accept my request, thus avoiding more bloodshed in this suffering country.*

*Thoughtfully,*
*Oscar A. Romero (Archbishop)*

## Appeal to Christian Democrats

I ask you to analyze not only your intentions, which are undoubtedly good, but also the real effects that your presence in the government is having. Your presence is concealing, especially at the international level, the repressive character of this regime. As a political force in our nation, you must take note of where your influence may be used most efficaciously on behalf of our poor. Do you wish to remain isolated and impotent, in a government dominated by repressive military officers? Or will you become one of several forces incorporated into the popular government? Such a government would take for its basis, not the armed forces, every day more corrupt, but instead the ideals of the majority of our nation.

I am not against the armed forces and their institutions. I continue to believe there are honest elements in the military; they are the only hope for the vindication of the military. I believe in the need for some true security corps to safeguard our nation. Nonetheless, I cannot agree with those military men who, making the worst possible use of their rank, are discrediting those necessary institutions, converting them into instruments of repression and injustice. They give the impression that law and order are supreme. This situation will continue as long as the government does not identify and punish those responsible for so much repression, and as long as it is unable to carry out the reforms proposed on behalf of the poor people. The oligarchy is taking advantage of the political weakness of the government to attack and impede it through military force, so that the reforms for the poor cannot be carried out.

More and more we hear, as before, the popular rumor of collusion between the security corps and clandestine armed groups. The sufferings of the nation continue; the nation cannot stand much more. For example, let me mention some violent acts directed against my beloved priests. Just as manure makes gardens grow, so calumny is making sanctity flower in our apostles out in the fields of pastoral ministry. We receive beautiful letters from priests who repudiate the calumny and make the authors of calumny responsible for what might occur to them. And they ratify their commitment to the people. They are not committed to anyone except

Christ and the people who reflect the holiness of Christ, our Lord.

Among the letters—too numerous to read—is one with information about the machine gun attack on the Jesuit fathers' residence. On Saturday, February 16, at 12:45 a.m., bursts from a G-3 and other machine guns were heard. About a hundred bullet holes were found in the outside doors of the home, inside on the first two floors and in a car. After the round of shots, a car was heard leaving at full speed.

The Jesuits who live in this residence have been persecuted for the last few years. Remember, in 1973 they were indicted for events in the St. Joseph Day School and the Jesuit priest Father Grande was assassinated. Other events show how this group of priests is hated and persecuted for what we have previously mentioned: for their commitment to the people.

Also 52 Jesuits were threatened where they work in Guatemala. The threat came as a reaction against the document they wrote in the name of all the Jesuits working in Central America denouncing the systematic abuse of power, economic injustice, the increase of indiscriminate violence and the grave violation of the human rights of the indigenous population of Guatemala.

Our magazine, *Busqueda,* which is highly recommended, contains an article about Father Rafael Palacios, assassinated on June 20 of last year, and Father Jose Alirio Napoleon Macias, assassinated on August 4. A compilation has been made of documents, testimonies and writings that demonstrate these priests were far from being communist infiltrators but were true messengers of the gospel of Jesus Christ.

I received a very sad letter from Juan Alcides Guardado, who spoke about his home in the housing complex of El Picacho, cantón La Laguna de Las Vueltas in Chalatenango. While he was traveling he was told not to go back home, that everything was destroyed. In fact, he was not even able to find his own mother. He asked me to issue a call through the radio station to see if his mother could be located so he could go to meet her. What terrible things happen in our country! Many have taken refuge in our cathedral; many are fleeing this wave of terrorism.

A letter from Mrs. Maria Ignacia Rivera, from San Agustin in Usulutan, tearfully denounced the assassination of her son Manuel de Jesús. His wife was left with six small children.

Professor Agustín Osmín Hernández was captured by five security agents on February 12 at 11:30 a.m. in Aguilares. His wife and the community of Zacamil are worried about him. I hope this announcement will speed his release or bring him before the courts, as is just.

Expressions of solidarity have come in, expressing regret over the machine gunning of Professor Guillermo Galvan's house.

Dr. Roberto Lara Velado has received threats on his life. Those who know his honorable ways cannot do less than stand in solidarity with him and denounce the threats on the life of this honorable Christian, Dr. Roberto Lara Velado.

The gravest danger comes from the extreme right. Much has been said about the possibility of a military attack from the right, as well as about a general strike of private companies. It would be unpardonable to stop the march of our people toward justice. Those who sustain the unjust order in which we live have no right to stage a revolt. Victory over a people already conscienticized would require much bloodshed and still would not be sufficient to drown the clamor for justice in the nation.

The most logical step is for the powers of the oligarchy, with human or Christian serenity if possible, to reflect on the call that Christ gives today in the gospel: "Woe to you, because tomorrow you shall weep!" As the familiar proverb says, it is much better to take off your rings in time, instead of having your hands cut off. Be logical; follow your human and Christian convictions; give the people a chance to organize; preserve a sense of justice. Do not try to defend what is indefensible.

Finally, let me say a word to the popular organizations. A fitting comment was made on our archdiocesan radio station YSAX: "The Revolutionary Coordinating Committee, as an instrument that promotes the unity of the people, makes efforts to consolidate (people); it attempts to dialogue with the democratic forces because it knows that without them its national projects will not be viable and might even be impossible. But what its leadership creates rationally and politically, its members destroy with acts of irrational fighting."

I want to say, then, that we should defend the right to organize, and we praise attempts at unity and openness. But we repudiate the tactics certain groups use. They either proceed without consulting their leaders or are ill-advised.

It is difficult to give credibility to those who think they can achieve reason and justice by means of irrational acts and unnecessary, violent actions. Agitation for agitation's sake is unproductive; violent measures do not build unity in any way.

I want to remind you that our Christian morality gives us this principle: trying to pressure someone else into consent, contract or compromise diminishes freedom greatly; therefore, one is not obliged to do something under such pressure. It is worth much more, then, to dialogue. If our popular organizations are truly maturing, they will show their maturity in dialoguing, not in doing irrational things.

I repeat my disapproval of the tactic of occupying buildings. It causes many inconveniences. I am a witness to the suffering of many hostages and their relatives, above all when the hostages suffer an illness that requires care. And in all cases, with what right is a human being denied freedom?

This attitude turns ridiculous and dangerous when two organizations compete to take over the same building. Such was the case here at the cathedral when FAPU wanted to move into the cathedral during BPR's occupancy, and **BPR** officials returned to discuss the occupation. FAPU members abused even the sacred vestments and they left albs and other vestments scattered everywhere. The new occupants had the dignity to clean up a little at least.

The occupation of the Salvadorean Institute of Foreign Trade by the **BPR** doesn't favor the unity that organizations seek, especially when Fenastras had already raised the salaries of the APLAR workers in the free zone of San Bartolo, and the reopening of the factory as a Salvadorean enterprise was being renegotiated. For this business transaction a trip was being planned to the United States today or tomorrow. Now that transaction cannot be completed because the lawyer Arturo Guzman Trigueros is held hostage and the directors cannot be found to dialogue about this problem. I urge **BPR** to reconsider this wrong move and in the name of 600 workers who might lose their jobs to do everything possible so Fenastras can continue with plans for the good of these workers.

Similar immaturity was shown by those who took over UCA: there was no possibility of dialoguing with the responsible people. That is why the rector could say, "What more can I say when I have already been dialoguing with these people for 22 hours?"

In the name of the religious sentiments of my people, for the good of the poor and of my people, I beg the directors of the organizations that today are occupying church buildings to come by to dialogue with me or with those responsible for the buildings. We hope to reopen them for the people's worship during Lent, which is drawing near. These buildings are temples of prayer for our people, whose Christian sentiments deserve at least as much consideration as the objectives of those occupying the buildings. The need to negotiate is urgent.

If the security forces would keep their distance from the churches, it would be easier for the churches to offer refuge to the people of the city. Remember, it has always been the church's mission to offer itself in every type of charity, not only in the church itself but in all its institutions. That is why I say that there is a need for dialogue. Don't think you have discovered something new when already the church is old in doing deeds of mercy and hospitality.

I also issue to the popular military organizations a call to return to the respectable paths of rationality, of human dignity. I am referring to the abductions, threats and exacting of vengeance. No one can render justice by their own hands; instead, they must appeal to the tribunals of justice. I am making many requests to those who are in a position to do something about lives that are in danger. Past crimes or sins do not matter when one speaks about the dignity of people. The pope has also said that violence cannot be inflicted, not even on those whom someone judges blameworthy, because it ends as vengeance.

Mr. Rodolfo Useda Franco from Ilobasco asked me to intervene for him because he was charged with helping attack the church in Los Dasamparados and has re-

ceived threatening phone calls. He denies that participation.

Also many neighbors from the canton La Loma de
San Pedro, Perulapan, proclaim their innocence; they
were accused over radio of having committed offenses
and having killed and buried people. They say these
charges are false.

Concerning the abduction of Mr. Dunn: a letter from
Argentina arrived in which the writer offered himself as
hostage in Mr. Dunn's place. All this would be unnecessary if the protagonists in these actions had human feelings. The fight for the people should ennoble every effort; it loses its virtue when it tramples over persons.

We conclude, then, as we have begun, saying that in
the poor, in the nation that suffers, there is a great ray of
hope. The church, in the name of Jesus Christ, wants to
root out all that is shameful in the nation.

Look at it this way. My effort to denounce is for no
other reason than to say this: we want a holy people, we
want a government that truly understands the poor, we
want a political system that truly promotes the well-
being of our people and of our poor. And thus we can
repeat today with Jesus Christ, "Happy the poor, because theirs is the kingdom of heaven!"

March 23, 1980
# The Church: Defender of Human Dignity

*Isaiah 43:16-21*
*Philippians 3:8-14*
*John 8:1-11*

## Introduction

We greet you beloved brothers and sisters visiting El Salvador on an ecumenical mission to study the state of human rights in our country. We are delighted you will share with us in this celebration of God's word and the eucharist.

Concelebrating this mass with me are Franciscan Father Alan McCoy, president of the U.S. Conference of Major Religious Superiors of Men, and Father Juan Macho Merino. Also present is Mr. Thomas Quigley, layman of the Latin American section of the Department of Social Development and World Peace of the U.S. Catholic Conference. Present too are: the Rev. William Wipfler of the program for human rights of the National Council of Churches in the United States; Mrs. Betty de Nute Richardson of the American Friends Service Committee, also in the U.S.; and Mr. Ronald Joung of the peace education program of the same service committee.

We sense in you, our visitors, the sympathy of North America. Because of that sympathy, we understand how the gospel can illuminate various types of societies. One feels solidarity with a church that clearly tries to defend the human rights that are trampled in our country. That solidarity exists because of the respect for human beings our Lord revealed to us.

Our thanks to our visitors. May the days you spend with us be extremely beneficial in further strengthening your Christian commitment. In our understanding of other countries, let us see how our efforts are understood and supported by all of those who are illuminated by the light of the gospel.

Greetings to the listeners of YSAX, our archdiocesan radio station, an instrument of truth and justice. You have long awaited this transmission, and the moment has now arrived, thanks be to God. We know the danger that threatens our poor radio station for being an instrument of truth and justice, but we know the risk must be taken, because an entire people depend on it as they strive to uphold this word of truth and justice.

Greetings also to the listeners of Radio News of the Continent. I am glad to have the collaboration of Radio News. It is carrying our voice from this microphone and through our transmitter to Latin America. Reporter Demetrio Olaziregui is here with us. He told us how a bomb exploded near the studios of the broadcasting station in Costa Rica. Dynamite charges destroyed part of the wall and blew out the windows of a two-story building. For a short time the station had to go off the

air, but it has resumed operations and is performing a
marvelous service for us. We are told our homilies will
continue to be broadcast since there is demand for them
in Venezuela, in Colombia, and from as far away as
Brazil. The radio station has received between 300 and
400 letters showing that people hear this broadcast perfectly in Honduras, in Nicaragua, and right here in El
Salvador, in many parts of our country.

## Lent, preparation for Easter

Giving thanks to God helps one's message reach
people. This is true even with a message which isn't
meant to be more than a modest reflection of the divine
word. If a person is thankful, the person's message gets
a marvelous reception because it touches people. And
the thankful proclamation of a message, in the context
of Lent, prepares people for Easter, an Easter that is a
shout of victory. No one can extinguish the life which
Christ revived. Not even death or hatred of him and his
church will overcome this life. Christ is the victor.

Holy Week is the celebration of redemption: Christ
will be glorified in an Easter of unending resurrection.
But we have to accompany him in Lent, in a Holy Week
that makes his cross, sacrifice and martyrdom real for
us. Christ is saying to us: "Happy are those who are not
offended by their cross."

Lent is, then, a call to celebrate our redemption in the
complex relationship of cross and victory. Our people
have the qualifications for this, because our surround-
ings preach to us of the cross. But those who have

Christian faith and hope know that behind this Calvary of El Salvador is our Easter, our resurrection, and that is the hope of the Christian people.

God's word in Lent reveals his plan to free humanity completely. During these Sundays of Lent, I have tried to disclose gradually God's plan to save nations and peoples that we learn about from divine revelation, from the word proclaimed here at mass. Today, different historical solutions are proposed for our people. We can be sure that victory will go to the one that best reflects God's plan. The church's mission is to help that victory along. That is why, in light of the divine word that reveals God's plan for people's happiness, we have the duty, dear brothers and sisters, to point out facts that show how the plan of God is being reflected or distorted in our midst.

Let no one be offended because we use the divine words read at our mass to illuminate the social, political and economic situation of our people. Not to do so would be un-Christian. Christ desires to unite himself with humanity, so that the light he brings from God might become life for nations and individuals.

I know many are shocked by this preaching and want to accuse us of forsaking the gospel for politics. But I reject this accusation. I am trying to bring to life the message of the Second Vatican Council and the meetings at Medellin and Puebla. The documents from these meetings should not just be studied theoretically. They should be brought to life and translated into the real struggle to preach the gospel as it should be for our people. Each week I go about the country collecting the cries of the people, their pain from so much crime, and the ignominy of so much violence. Each week I ask the Lord to give me the right words to console, to denounce, to call for repentance. And even though I may be a voice crying in the desert, I know that the church is making the effort to fulfill its mission.

Here's a summary of that plan of God we've heard on these Lenten Sundays:

— Christ is the way. For that reason, he is presented to us fasting and conquering temptations in the desert. Christ is the goal and the impetus of life; because of that, he appeared to us transfigured, to call us to that goal to which everyone is called.

— The collaboration of humanity is conversion. On the other Sundays of Lent—the third and fourth—we learned that God asks people to collaborate with him to be saved. The collaboration that God asks of people is conversion, reconciliation with him. In the precious examples of the fruitless fig tree, of the prodigal son, and from this morning's example of the adulteress who repents and is pardoned, comes the invitation God gives to us. He tells us that we will find ourselves forgiven just as the father forgave the prodigal son, just as the Savior forgave the adulteress. No sin goes unpardoned; hatred can be reconciled when we convert and sincerely return to the Lord. That is the message of Lent!

God's plan is realized in history. The readings of Lent tell us how God applied his "project" to history in order to make the people's history a story of their salvation. Insofar as those peoples reflect the plan of God—to save us in Christ by conversion—they gain salvation and happiness. For that reason, the history of Israel is treated in the first reading for each Sunday of Lent. The Israelites are a paradigm people, an example even in their infidelities and sins, because from them we learn how God punished infidelities and sins. They are also the model of how God brings about the promise of salvation. We travel with Moses on the pilgrimage through the desert; with Joshua, we arrive to celebrate the first Easter in the promised land.

And today, we are invited to a second exodus: the return from Babylon. This is a story each nation has to imitate. Every population may not be the same as Israel's but one element does exist in all peoples: a group that follows Christ. The people of God are not the entire population, naturally, but a group of the faithful.

The example of Israel returning from Babylon is precious to us this morning, when followers of Christ in the U.S. have come to share with the followers of Christ here in El Salvador. Christians in the great nation to the north are the voice of the gospel against that society's injustices. They come to stand beside us in solidarity so that we, the people of God here in El Salvador, may also know how to denounce with courage the injustices of our own society.

In light of today's divine word, I am going to present a reflection on this theme: "the church, a servant of personal, communitarian and transcendent liberation."

These are the three main thoughts of today's homily: human dignity is the first thing freedom demands; God wants to save all peoples; and transcendence gives liberation its true and definitive dimension.

## The dignity of the person

Look at the gospel. I find no more beautiful example of Jesus safeguarding human dignity than this sinless Jesus face to face with an adulteress, humiliated because she has been caught in adultery. Her judges sentence her to be stoned to death. Jesus silently reproaches her judges in their sin, asks the woman, "Has no one condemned you?"

"No one, Lord."

"Well, neither do I condemn you, but sin no more."

Christ has strength and tenderness. He puts human dignity before all. There was a legal problem in the time of Christ. According to Deuteronomy, every woman caught in adultery was to die. When it came time to discuss how that death ought to be effected, the pharisees and the lawyers debated: "By stoning, by strangulation?" And they referred the question to Jesus: "This woman has been caught in adultery. Our law says that she ought to die. What do *you* say? According to the present discussion, how should we kill her?"

These legal details were not important to Jesus. In answer to the bad will of those laying a trap for him, Jesus began to write in the sand in an aimless way, like doodling on paper with a pencil. They insisted on an answer and Jesus gave them the great answer from his teaching: "Let the one among you who is without sin be the first to throw a stone."

He touched their consciences. According to the ancient laws, they were witnesses, the ones that should have thrown the first stone. But in examining their consciences, the witnesses found they were witnesses of their own sins. So the dignity of the woman is saved. God does not save sin, but the dignity of a woman submerged in sin. Yes, God does save that. Jesus loves sinners; he has come precisely to save them, and here is an example of his doing that. To convert the adulteress is much better than to stone her; to pardon her and save her are much better than to condemn her. The law has to promote human dignity and must not use false legalities to trample upon the integrity of persons.

The gospel records the spontaneous reaction of the crowd: "They started to fall away, beginning with the oldest." Life is spent offending God, and the years slip by that ought to strengthen our commitment, to humanity, to human dignity, to God. We become more and more hypocritical, hiding the sins that increase along with age.

Personal sin is the root of great social sins. Dear brothers and sisters, we must be very clear on this point because today it is very easy, as it was for the witnesses against the adulteress, to point out one sinner and yet to beg justice for others. But how few look at their own consciences! How easy it is to denounce structural injustice, institutionalized violence, social sin! All that is a reality, but where are the roots of that social sin? In the heart of every human being. Today's society is a kind of anonymous world in which no one wants to take the blame and everyone is responsible. Everyone is responsible for social sin, but its source is anonymous. We are all sinners and we have all added our grain of sand to the massive crime and violence in our country.

For that reason, salvation begins with the human person, with human dignity, with freeing every person from sin. And in Lent, this is God's call: be converted, individually! There are no two identical sinners among us. Each one of us has committed his or her own shameful deeds, yet we want to lay the blame on the other and hide our own faults. I must unmask myself. I, too, am one of them, and I need to beg God's pardon because I have offended him and society. This is the call of Christ: the human person comes before all else!

How beautiful is the expression of that woman upon finding herself pardoned and understood. "No one, Lord. No one has condemned me."

"Then neither do I, I who could give that truly condemning word, neither do I condemn. But be careful. Do not sin again." Do not sin again! Let us be careful, brothers and sisters. Since God has forgiven us so many times, let us take advantage of that friendship with the Lord which we have recovered and let us live it gratefully.

A note on the advancement of women: how beautifully a chapter on the promotion of woman by Christianity would fit in here! If she has achieved heights

similar to man's much of this is due to the gospel of
Jesus Christ. In the time of Christ, people were shocked
that he would speak to a Samaritan woman because a
woman was considered unworthy to speak to a man.
Jesus knows that we are all equal, that there is no longer Greek nor Jew, man nor woman. We are all children of God. Women should be doubly appreciated by
Christianity because Christ is the one who has encouraged the greatness of women. What heights women are
capable of, when they use those feminine gifts that are
often neither encouraged nor appreciated because of
the machismo of men.

The witnesses must also understand that salvation
begins with human dignity. Before being judges who
administer justice, they have to be honest people who
can pass sentence with a clean conscience because they
would be the first to apply it to themselves if they were
to commit that crime.

Jesus' attitude is what we must focus on in this gospel, what we must learn. A sensitivity toward the person, however sinful that person may be, is what distin-
guishes him as the Son of God, the image of the Father.
He does not condemn, but pardons. However, he does
not tolerate sin. He is strong in rejecting sin, but he
knows how to condemn the sin and save the sinner. He
does not subordinate the person to the law. And this is
very important in our own times. He says, "The human
person was not made for the Sabbath, but the Sabbath
was made for humanity."

Let us not call upon our country's constitution to

defend our acts of selfishness, using it for our own interests. The law has already been abused everywhere. The law is for the benefit of the human person, not the person for the law. Jesus has given human dignity its rightful place, and we feel peace in that fact. We feel that we can count on Jesus, that we are not bound by sin, that we can repent and return to Jesus with sincerity. This is the deepest joy of being human.

In today's second reading, we have another example of a sinner who went about fooling himself for a long time. But in coming to know Christ he was saved and placed all his dreams, the aim of his whole life, in Christ.

"And everything else has become as nothing to me," the epistle says to us today. When the things of earth are no longer idolized, when we know the true God, the true Savior, then all earthly ideologies, all worldly strategies, all the idols of power, of money, of material possessions become as nothing to us. St. Paul uses an even stronger word, "manure." He says, "As long as I can win Christ, all the rest seems like manure to me."

When we bishops met in Puebla, we issued a statement on the human person. So as not to keep you too long, brothers and sisters, I won't read the whole rich content of the Puebla document on the theological foundations of the dignity of persons. Let me just discuss three theological themes from Puebla: the truth about Christ; the truth about the church; and the truth about the human person.

As bishops of the continent we signed a document

there, committing ourselves to promoting the human person. We spoke about the false earthly visions which make the human person an instrument of exploitation, or those visions in Marxist ideologies which make the person but a cog in the machinery, or those visions promoting national security which make the person a servant of the state, as if the state were lord and humanity the slave, when the reverse is true. Humanity does not exist for the state, but rather the state exists for humanity. The ideal of promoting the person must be the highest aim of all human organization.

We, the bishops of Latin America, have committed ourselves: "We profess, then, that every man and every woman, no matter how insignificant they may seem, have within themselves an inviolable nobility that they and all others ought to respect unconditionally; that each human life deserves to be treated with dignity for its own sake, under whatever circumstance; that all human coexistence has to be based on the common good, on the realization of the increasingly severe reprimand the common dignity makes against injustice. The common dignity does not permit using some persons for the pleasure of others, but demands that people should be prepared to sacrifice particular goods."

This is the basis of our sociology, that which we learn from Christ in his gospel: before all else, the human being is what we have to save, and individual sin is the first thing we have to correct. Our personal accounts before God, our individual relationship with him, set the stage for everything else. False liberators are people whose souls are slaves to sin but who clamor for justice. They are often cruel because they know neither how to love nor how to respect the human person.

## God wants to save everyone

In moving from the individual to the communitarian, we come to the second theme for this homily. The idea is presented beautifully in today's readings, which show how God desires to save people as a group. It is the whole population God wants to save.

Today's first reading, the famous poem of Isaiah, presents God speaking with a people. Isaiah records the dialogue of God with what is called a "corporate personality," as though God were speaking with one person. God speaks with a people and to that people. God makes them his people because he is going to entrust them with promises, revelations that soon will serve for all peoples.

There is a difference between "people of God" and all people. Mark my words, beloved brothers and sisters: in the Bible, there are things that apply only to the "people of God," and there are also some things that apply to people in general, to all people. How many times the prophets reproached Israel for delighting in being children of Abraham without obeying and believing in God. The believers, that diminished number, were the true people of God. At times, all the rest were corrupt and so, too, were the other people who were called the Gentiles. But that nucleus called the people of God, the corporate person with whom God speaks, works through Christ to make all people Christians.

No longer is there only one group of people of God from Israel; now there are also many groups of people of God.

Here this morning we have an example. There is a group of Christians in the United States that does not include all people there, just as in El Salvador there is a group of Christians that does not include all of El Salvador's people. And when I, as pastor, address the people of God, I don't pretend to be the master of all of El Salvador. I am the servant of a nucleus that is called the church, the archdiocese, those that want to serve Christ and who recognize the bishop as the teacher who speaks to them in the name of Christ.

I feel so united with this core group of Christians that it doesn't bother me that those who are not of the church, although some may be within it, criticize me, murmur at me, pick me apart. They are no longer the people of God. This is in line with the New Testament. Even though they may be baptized, even though they may come to mass, if they can't join in solidarity with the exacting teachings of the gospel and the concrete applications of our pastoral letter, then, brothers and sisters, we know well how to discern these unfaithful people so as not to cheapen that sacred name: the people of God. We appeal to the people of God, to the nucleus of Salvadoreans who believe in Christ and who want to follow him faithfully, and who are nourished by his life, his sacraments and his pastors.

## God saves in history

This people of God exists throughout history. Did

you notice what today's reading says so beautifully?
"You were glorified by the first exodus, when I took
you out of Egypt, when you crossed the desert. How
many marvelous deeds were done on that journey with
Moses! But glory no longer in that past! Already, that
has become history. I make all things new." What a
beautiful phrase from God! It is God who makes all
things new; it is God who goes on in history.

Isaiah says the exodus will now come from another
direction, from Babylon, from exile. The desert through
which the people are going to pass will flower like a
garden; the waters will gush forth, symbolizing the giving of God's pardon. The people will be reconciled
with God on the way to Jerusalem. The exodus is no
longer from the slavery of Egypt, but from the desert of
Babylon. And so history will go on unfolding.

Every country lives its own "exodus"; today El Salvador is living its own exodus. Today we are passing to
our liberation through a desert strewn with bodies and
where anguish and pain are devastating us. Many suffer the temptation of those who walked with Moses and
wanted to turn back and not work together. It is the
same old story. God, however, wants to save the people
by making a new history. History does not repeat itself,
although there is a saying to that effect. Obviously,
there are certain phenomena that are repeated. What is
not a repetition of past history is the circumstance, the
precise moment to which we are witnesses in El Salvador.

How complicated is our history, how varied from

one day to another! One leaves El Salvador and returns the following week, and it seems that the history of the country has changed completely. Let us not judge things as we once judged them. One thing is important: let us keep our faith in Jesus Christ, the God of history, firmly anchored in the soul. That does not change. But Christ has, as it were, the satisfaction of changing history, of influencing history: "I make all things new."

The grace of the Christian, therefore, must not be based on traditions that no longer sustain themselves, but must apply that eternal tradition of Christ to the present realities. We have to have changes in the church, dear brothers and sisters, a fact that applies above all to those of us who have been formed at other times, in other systems. We have to ask God for the grace to adapt ourselves without betraying our faith, to understand the present moment. God makes all things new. He punished the Israelites because, glorying in the first exodus, they did not think God could perform marvels in a second exodus or that he would do greater things in the Christian era, as we ourselves are seeing.

History will not cease; God sustains it. That is why I say that insofar as historical projects attempt to reflect the eternal plan of God, to that extent they reflect the kingdom of God. This attempt is the work of the church. Because of this, the church, the people of God in history, is not settled in any one social system, in any political organization, in any party. The church does not identify herself with any of those forces because she is the eternal pilgrim of history and is indicating at every historical moment what reflects the kingdom of God and what does not reflect the kingdom of God. She is the servant of the kingdom of God.

The great task of Christians must be to absorb the spirit of God's kingdom and, with souls filled with the kingdom of God, to work on the projects of history. It's fine to be organized in popular groups; it's all right to form political parties; it's all right to take part in the government. It's fine as long as you are a Christian who carries the reflection of the kingdom of God and tries to establish it where you are working, and as long as you are not being used to further worldly ambitions. This is the great duty of the people of today.

My dear Christians, I have always told you, and I will repeat, that the true liberators of our people must come from us Christians, from the people of God.

Any historical plan that's not based on what we spoke of in the first point—the dignity of the human being, the love of God, the kingdom of Christ among people—will be a fleeting project. Your project, however, will grow in stability the more it reflects the eternal design of God. It will be a solution for the common good of the people every time, if it meets the needs of the people.

We must be grateful for the church, dear political brothers and sisters, and not manipulate the church into saying what we want; instead, we must speak out for what the church teaches. The church doesn't have interests. I do not have any ambition for power. Because of that, I freely tell the powerful people what is good and what is bad. I also tell any political group what is good and what is bad. That is my duty.

Having that freedom of the kingdom of God, we, the church (which is not only the bishop and the priests, but all of you, the faithful, the religious, the Catholic schools, all who are the people of God, the nucleus of believers in Christ), should unify our efforts. We should not divide ourselves or appear dispersed. Many times it's as though we are influenced too much by popular political organizations, and we want to please them, rather than work for the kingdom of God in its eternal designs. We don't have to lie to anyone because we have much to give everyone. This is not arrogance, but the grateful humility of people who have received a revelation from God to communicate to others.

## Transcendence and liberation

Finally, the third thought taken from today's readings is that the plan of God for liberating his people is transcendent.

I think I may repeat this idea too often, but I'll never tire of saying it because we often run the risk of wanting to get out of present situations with immediate resolutions, and we forget that quick answers can be bandaids, not true solutions. The true solution has to fit into the definitive plan of God. Every effort we make for better land distribution, for better administration of wealth in El Salvador, for a political organization structured around the common good of Salvadoreans, will always have to be made within the context of definitive liberation.

Recently, I was taught a very important theory. It is that one who works in politics looks at temporal problems such as money, land and things, and is content with simply solving these problems. But the politician who has faith goes to God, and from God's point of view looks at that immediate problem which the politicians are trying to solve. The problem should not be considered apart from God's perspective.

From the beginning to the end of history, God has a plan; for any solution to be effective, it must be molded according to that perspective of God. And according to God's perspective, as it appears in today's readings from the Bible, three things are clear: in the first place, we must recognize God as the protagonist of history; in the second place, we must break out of bondage to sin; and in the third place, we must not reject Christ, who is the way and the goal of true liberation. There it is in today's readings. This is the plan we have been studying through Lent.

First, we must recognize God's initiative in order to liberate our people. Today's readings clearly show that God is the one who takes the initiative. In the first reading, God speaks of "the people that I formed." It is God speaking with Israel: "I chose you: I am making your history for you." The moment we understand that we are no more than instruments of God is a beautiful one.

Whatever lives comes from God. We can do only as much as God wants us to do; we have only as much intelligence as God has given us. We must place all those limitations in God's hands and recognize that without God we can do nothing. My beloved brothers and sisters, with that sense of transcendence, we are called to pray much, to be very united with God at this hour in El Salvador. There are people who are working for liberation by uniting themselves with God.

The other day we were speaking about the problem of the refugee camp. Do not confuse the refugee camp with a barracks; the refugee camp is for people who come with fear and who come fleeing, trying to hide themselves. Some of them say, "Well, we're organized, we can't freeload, we want to work." Fine, go to work, look for a place to work.

The refugee camp is full of sick people. There was a man with his sick wife and their children, who really lacked the strength to work, and they wanted to include that family in the takeover of a church. And how is she going to do this if she is sick? She can offer her pain and sickness. This has value. But when one loses sight of the transcendence of the struggle, all that is done consists of transitory actions that are themselves wrong at times. I wish that all those who labor for the liberation of humanity would realize that without God one can do nothing, and that with God, even the most useless work is valuable when done with good intent.

In today's first reading, God invites the people of Israel to discover his hand, not only in their exodus from Egypt to the promised land, but also in their return from Babylon to Jerusalem. To see the hand of God in the historical reality of that people is to experience transcendence. Those who work—I repeat—for the liberation of the people should not lose sight of this transcendent dimension.

The second point about the transcendent nature of liberation is this: we must remember that liberation must free us from sin. We must bear in mind that all evils have a common root. It is sin. In the human heart are egotism, envy, idolatry, and from these come divisions and avarice. As Christ said, "It is not what comes out of persons that defiles them, but rather what is in the human heart: evil thoughts."

We must purify, then, that source of all bondage. Why are there chains? Why are there "marginal" people? Why is there illiteracy? Why are there diseases? Why do people mourn in pain? All of that indicates that sin does exist. "The poverty of a people," says Medellín, "is a denunciation of the injustice that people endures."

Liberation, because it is transcendent, lifts us from our sins. The church will always be preaching, "Repent of your personal sins." And she will say, as Christ did to the adulteress, "I do not condemn you; you have repented, but do not sin again." Brothers and sisters, all of you who think little of an intimate relationship with God, how much I want to convince you how important God is! It is not enough to say, I'm an atheist, or I don't believe in God, or I don't offend him. It is not a question of what you believe. Objectively you have broken with the source of life. As long as you don't discover this, don't follow him, and don't love him, you are cut off from your creator. And because of this, you carry within yourself disorder, disunity, ingratitude, lack of faith, lack of community. Without God, there is no true liberation. Granted, one may achieve temporary liberations. But definitive, lasting liberations—only people of faith are going to realize them.

The third idea on the transcendent aspect of liberation is that transcendence asks of us great faith in Jesus Christ. Today's second reading gives us an incomparable page from the life of St. Paul, the sinner who had forgotten Christ or, rather, did not know him and believed instead that Christ and his Christians were traitors of the true religion, Judaism. Paul felt authorized to persecute them, arrest them and finish them off.

But when Christ revealed himself to Paul, Paul understood his own ignorance. Thus he wrote, "All that I esteemed I now count as loss compared to the excellence of knowing Jesus Christ, my Lord." What gratitude from a sinner! Paul says, "I didn't know you, Lord; now, yes, now I know you and now all the rest seems useless to me compared to the excellence of knowing you, my Lord! For Christ, I lost everything. And all I esteemed I count as refuse, in order that I may gain Christ and be found in him, not having righteousness of my own but with that justice which comes from faith in Christ." This is transcendence.

There are many who want justice, their own justice, a simple human justice. They do not go beyond that. That is not what saves me, says St. Paul; rather, justice comes from faith in Christ, my Lord. And how is Christ judge of humanity? St. Paul hopes "to know Christ and the strength of his resurrection and to share his sufferings, becoming like him in his death that I may attain one day the resurrection of the dead."

Do you see how life recovers all of its meaning? Do you see how suffering becomes a communion with the Christ who suffers, and death becomes a communion with the death that redeemed the world? Who can feel worthless before this treasure that one finds in Christ, that gives meaning to sickness, to pain, to oppression and repression? Whoever believes in Christ, even under the oppressor's boot, knows that he or she is a victor and that the definitive victory will be that of truth and justice!

In the same intimate passage, St. Paul says, "The most important thing is not what I've alrady acquired, but rather that I rush forward, forgetting what remains behind and flinging myself toward that which is ahead. I run toward the goal in order to win the prize of God's heavenly call in Jesus Christ." This is transcendence: the goal toward which we strive with each step of liberation, a goal that is definitive joy for all people.

## Events of the week

Brothers and sisters, this trancendent liberation is the liberation our church has to live and preach. We have already learned it from the word of God on the eve of Holy Week. And we are going to enter into Holy Week forming ourselves more into the church, the people of God.

I speak at this moment to my beloved priests, to the religious communities, to the Christian communities, to all who are called the church, the people of God, the nucleus of believers, in order that from here, from this core of believers, we might have the strength (as God gave it to Israel) to enlighten all other peoples, to illuminate and denounce that which is not good, and to encourage all that is good. For that reason, at this point in my homily, I am directing myself to the task of our church, asking of all church workers to truly make the church a vehicle of the liberation called for in the plan of God.

The first thing I announce to you today is that next Sunday we begin Holy Week. Because of special circumstances we are going to celebrate it here, in the basilica. At 8 a.m. next Sunday, we'll have the blessing of the palms. We hope to combine our service with that of the Church of Calvary. In that case, I am asking you to be in the Church of Calvary at about 7:30 a.m. where we will bless the palms. From there, we will have a procession—which symbolizes the triumphal entrance of Christ into Jerusalem—to the entrance of the basilica to celebrate Palm Sunday mass.

The rest of the events of Holy Week will appear on the program. The first major celebration comes on Holy Thursday, with the blessing of the oils at 10 a.m., but we will announce all of this next Sunday. I only want to tell you ahead of time that we would like to give our Good Friday Way of the Cross its full meaning of amendment, of denunciation and of solidarity, the three attitudes with which a Christian should meditate on the passion of Christ. We live among a people who shoulder their own heavy cross. Next Sunday, we will give you the details for this celebration of the great Way of the Cross that is truly one with the way of the cross of our own people.

Let me mention various communities in the archdiocese. As I already told you last Sunday, the celebration of the feast of St. Joseph proved to be very prayerful in San José de la Montaña, in the seminaries under his patronage, in San José Cortes, in San José Villanueva, in Christopher Columbus Academy—directed by the Josephine fathers—and in the St. Joseph day school.

In Aguilares, we celebrated the third anniversary of Father Rutilio Grande's assassination. The repression is obviously having its effect—few people were present; there is fear. One could say the people of Aguilares are being martyred. The message was that Christ's messenger will always find what Father Grande found, if the messenger is faithful.

In Tejutla, in the village of Los Martinez, we celebrated the village feast day. And there they told me of a terrible violation of human rights. On March 7 about midnight, a truckful of soldiers, some in mufti and some in uniform, opened doors, entered homes, and rousted all the members of each family, violently kicking them and beating them with rifle butts. The soldiers raped four young women, savagely beat up their parents, and threatened that if they said anything about it they would have to bear the consequences. We have learned of the tragedy of these poor young girls.

In Agua Caliente, we had a beautiful confirmation ceremony—the people are very kind there in the district of Chalatenango, in the parish of Mary our Queen.

In Cojutepeque, the parish priest, Father Richard Ayala, has been the victim of a false denunciation. This telegram arrived at the chancery, a copy of a telegram from the director of the National Guard to the head of the general staff:

"I deem it an honor to forward to you this radio communication originating this date from the Cojutepeque National Guard. The communication reads, 'Major, Director of National Police, I am communicating by telephone that this headquarters has learned that toward the end of last week, Father Richard Ayala, parish priest of San Sebastian Church in this city, met with groups of people of both sexes in the village of San Andres, in the jurisdiction of Monte San Juan in this district, to report to them that on the 15th of this month he will leave for Nicaragua or for Cuba to bring reinforcements to continue the revolt in our country.' " The major signed the telegram.

Ridiculous, right?

When we called on Father Ayala, whom many know for his seriousness, he wrote this directive to the engineer Duarte, who sent the telegram to me at the curia: "On the subject of the telegram, I tell you this: first, it is true that on the date indicated I was in the villages of El Carmen and Soledad in the jurisdiction of Monte San Juan, and I was accompanied by Father Benjamín Rodríguez, a parish priest from that area; second, our visit was intended to reconcile and console both factions with religious words and the gospel; and third, it is completely false and biased to assert that we may have offered to leave the country on the 15th of the present month to bring back reinforcements from other countries in order to continue the fight. That is *not* our language, nor is that the pastoral mission to which we have entrusted ourselves. Sincerely, Father Ayala.''

In another community of the Cuscatlán district, in Candelaria, it is reported that the National Guard in the villages of San Miguel, Nance Verde and San Juan Miraflores Arriba—with the understanding of officials in Candelaria, Cuscatlán—in the afternoon hours arrested a young reservist, Emilio Mejía, who was riding a bus with other people toward Cojutepeque.

He was taken to his village, San José La Ceiba, where that same afternoon he was killed in front of the house of Don Salvador Mejía. There his body was picked up by his mother, Doña Carmen Martinez de Mejía, on the morning of the following day and he was buried that afternoon. Some say that this happened by mistake; the police were looking for another person with the same name. Fatal mistake.

Second, Mr. Emilio Mejía was arrested in his own home in the village of San Juan Miraflores Arriba, in front of his wife, Doña Pilar Raymundo de Mejía, and after being abused, he was taken from the house. The following day, his wife found him about two blocks away, decapitated.

Third, arrested in their home in the village of San

Miguel Nance Verde were Don José Cupertino Alvarado and his daughters, Carmen Alvarado and María Josefa Alvarado. They were found dead on a coffee plantation behind the chapel in the village of San Juan Miraflores Arriba. The following day, they were buried in a common grave by their relatives.

Fourth, it is on record that all of the dead were arrested while peacefully abiding in their homes—with the exception of the first one (young Emilio Mejía)—without offering resistance. The signer of this statement saw a bus full of National Guardsmen in front of the ANTEL office in the afternoon hours.

The statement offers a beautiful legal analysis; the signer makes it very clear that the law, in addition to people's lives, has been trampled upon. One of his paragraphs says, "With the present declaration, I am not defending anarchy or subversion if in fact the dead have been accused of such things, but rather I am calling into question this lawless conduct completely opposed to the dignity of human persons."

In response to our chancery's protest of the seizure of the Belgian fathers' house on the Zacamil settlement, the Ministry of Defense has answered, "As regards the seizure of the house named, I want to offer the following details for your consideration: first, that it has no sign to identify it as the house of priests or as a place of religious worship; second, that not only was that house seized but also another in the same area because there were reports that merited investigation—that is to say, that the second house seized was supect, as was that of the fathers. . . ; third, that as soon as it was verified that the house belonged to priests and that nothing suspicious was found, the seizure was suspended; fourth, that the possibility is not being dismissed that after the seizures other persons may have entered the house interested in doing damage or in leaving the appearance that the seizure was violent.

"I admit that upon questioning the members of the National Guard about the incident at hand, they did not deny that the seizure was carried out. We ordered them to have more care and consideration for special cases like the one noted, and ordered that we be consulted before they act." The events tell us another story!

The following announcements will help keep you informed about the life of our diocese. We will have confirmations at 4 p.m. today on Real Ciudad Delgado Street.

This week, the catechumenal communities will celebrate the coming of Easter.

In Soyapango, a new Christian center, directed by the Dominican Fathers of the Rosary, has been opened.

In Santa Tecla, the church's basic community studies and commits itself more and more to its pastoral activities.

In Chalatenango, a new parish is springing up: Christ the King Parish, formed to serve Paraíso, Aldeíta and Chalatenango. The pastor will be Father Gabriel Rodríguez. The parish will be staffed by four seminarians spending their diaconate year there, in preparation for their coming priesthood.

The education communities are also working pastorally in the Catholic academies. They are carrying out everyone's wish that the work of the schools parallel and not at all oppose the pastoral mission of the archdiocese. We had meetings with the lay people of the Assumption Academy, and we will have meetings with those of Sacred Heart Academy.

Two organizations in the diocese are renewing their staffs; they make up the pastoral council, along with nine vicars. Their first priority for two days this week was to study the archdiocesan pastoral plan that matches—and bear this in mind, so that you are not surprised later by misleading information—the thought of Vatican II, the gatherings at Medellin and Puebla, and the pastoral weeks that have been celebrated in our archdiocese.

I do not like it when people refer to the "thinking of the archbishop." I have no personal guidelines; rather, I try to follow the lessons of the great events of the church. And I am delighted that the pastoral commission studies documents such as the diocese's plan, which I already received, like a precious heritage, from Monsignor Chávez, a plan we are trying to put into practice. We are having great success with it in the communities that take it seriously.

The priests' senate also named its new board of directors. It is an organization that functions to serve every priest and the whole diocese.

This morning's broadcast is a special event for Father Pick and his collaborators who have worked so hard to get the broadcasting station working, the station that allows people from far away to listen to our message.

The gesture of solidarity made by our North American Christian brothers and sisters is not isolated. I have learned that in North America many statements from Christian groups expressed sympathy for the letter we sent to the president of the United States. These groups support our desire that he not give military help that contributes to the repression of our people.

One of those statements of support is an article signed by Mr. Murat Williams, who was U.S. ambassador here in El Salvador during the time of President Rivera. He confirms, from his experience, that such aid from the United States always ends up being used for military repression here in El Salvador.

Because there can be confusion about certain events, our secretary of information has prepared two clarifications.

The first one refers to the policeman tortured in the cathedral. The official version leaves the role of our archbishopric a little ambiguous. It says that people had recourse to the archbishopric and that the result was negative. This wording is dangerous; we never fail to pay attention when action is needed, and we always do what we can. The bulletin explains:

"On March 21, members of FAPU requested that the archbishopric help them with the burial of 17 bodies

that they had in the cathedral because they were afraid
of being stopped on the way to the cemetery. Because of
that, they had to bury the dead in the cathedral. The
archbishopric promised to obtain guarantees for the
burial. That was successfully carried out through the
Ministry of Defense, which paid close attention to the
case, arranging the participation of the International
Red Cross and requesting the participation of the Ministry of Public Health.

"The arrangements made on behalf of the archbishopric were communicated to the representatives of the
organizations, FAPU and BPR, but the representatives
disagreed on what action to take. Some favored taking
the dead to the cemetery and the others said they should
be buried in the cathedral. The representatives of the
archbishopric, as well as the members of the International Red Cross, said they would collaborate in a normal burial, but would not assist in the show of protest
that the organizations might be expected to make on
this occasion.

"When these arrangements were made, Colonel Rey-
naldo López Nuila, director of the National Police,
requested by telephone the intervention of the archbishopric so that the occupants of the cathedral would
free Corporal Miguel Angel Zúñiga, who had been
seized by them. The archbishop immediately sent a
delegate to the cathedral. The occupants paid the delegate no attention, and they denied having Corporal
Zúñiga there. Later, with a member of Legal Aid, the
delegate went to the University of El Salvador to speak
with the Revolutionary Coordinating Committee.

There, they were informed that the corporal's capture was a certainty but that they had not yet freed him. At the same time, with representatives of the International Red Cross, they talked about the burial of the bodies. In this discussion it was decided that the BPR would bury its members in the cemetery, and FAPU would bury its members in the cathedral.

"Secondly, a commission of priests and lay people presented themselves at the Military Hospital to speak with Corporal Miguel Angel Zúñiga. He told them that when he was passing in front of the cathedral, four individuals armed with submachine guns approached him. They brought him into the cathedral and carried him to the basement, where they beat him up and handcuffed him and gave him electrical shocks. They also gave him blows to the ears and stomach, demanding that he tell them the names of his superiors and companions, as well as the numbers of their vehicles. They said he should report all of this information to the national university.

"One of those who interrogated him sprayed his eyes with a sulfurous-smelling liquid that gave him great pain and fever. They threatened him if he didn't reveal what was done to the people of San Martín, and they said they were going to kill his mother. They held guns to his head. He swore to them by God and his mother that he had never tortured or done harm to anyone. At last, they pushed him out in the street where he hailed a taxi. The doctor that attended him at the hospital said that for the time being Corporal Zúñiga could not see, but that the doctors hoped he would regain his sight. Two of his fingers are paralyzed because of the electric shocks.''

This is what happened to the policeman. In no way did we approve something so cruel. Each human being is far more valuable than we know, and it is absolutely necessary to respect each person.

The other case we want to clarify it this: the Catholic church has opened four buildings on its property to shelter refugees who have fled their homes because of the violence afflicting many places in this country. Our church is fully aware that protecting with care anyone who suffers is one of its principal obligations; we should not take into account the person's creed or political persuasion or way of thinking. For the church, it is enough simply to know a person is coming for help.

The church has set aside four sites for refuge, not for centers of political indoctrination of any sort, and by no means for military training camps that put people in danger instead of protecting them. The church has asked popular organizations to respect the strict function of sheltering, the purpose that those places have assumed. This purpose has also been made known to the military authorities.

The church is carrying out this humanitarian work by means of Cáritas, the archbishopric's official organization for giving this kind of service. Aside from Cáritas, the church does not recognize any other organization as a charitable agency officially representing the church. It remains very clear, then, that only

Cáritas represents the archbishopric in these works of kindness, help and charity. Cáritas is a member of CEAH (Economic Committee of Humanitarian Aid) that unites, on an economic level, many organizations that have a social sensitivity. These other organizations, though, do not represent the Catholic church; it is represented only by Cáritas.

The archbishopric entrusts to Cáritas the duty of persevering in devoted intervention for the needy, through humanitarian and Christian endeavors. And if the efforts of Cáritas have not gained all the desired results, this has not been from inaction, but rather from not having found the understanding and the collaboration necessary.

On a pleasant note, let me mention something special done in our diocese: a composer and poet has written a beautiful hymn for us in honor of our divine Savior. Now, listen to some lines from it:

> *The explosive songs of joy vibrate.*
> *I am going to join myself*
> *with the people in the cathedral . . .*
> *thousands of voices, we unite ourselves*
> *   on this day*
> *to sing our patron's feast day.*

The hymn includes stanzas very sensitive to what our people are undergoing. The last stanza is beautiful:

> *But the gods of power and money*
> *are opposed to what transfiguration*
> *   may hold.*

> *Because of that, you support us now,*
> *Lord,*
> *our leader against oppression.*

I had some texts from the pope, which we are going to omit because I only brought them to confirm the doctrine we are preaching. Above all, the doctrine gives top priority to respect for the human being.

## National events

Now I invite you to share the church's perspective on various events. The church tries to be the kingdom of God on earth and so often must illuminate the realities of our national situation.

We have lived a tremendously tragic week. I could not give you the facts before, but a week ago Saturday, on March 15, one of the strongest and most distressing military operations was carried out in the countryside. The villages affected were La Laguna, Plan de Ocotes and El Rosario. The operation brought tragedy: a lot of ranches were burned, acts of plundering were committed, and—never avoided in such an operation—people were killed. In La Laguna, the attackers killed a married couple, Ernesto Navas and Audelia Mejía de Navas, their little children, Martin and Hilda, 13 and seven years old, and 11 more peasants.

Other deaths have been reported, but we do not know the names of the dead. In Plan de Ocotes, two children and four peasants were killed, including two women. In El Rosario, three more peasants were killed. That was last Saturday.

Last Sunday, the following were assassinated in Arcatao by four members of ORDEN: peasants Marcelino Serrano, Vincente Ayala, 24, and his son, Freddy. That same day, Fernando Hernández Navarro, a peasant, was assassinated in the village Calera de Jutiapa, when he fled from the military.

Last Monday, March 17, was a tremendously violent day. Bombs exploded in the capital as well as in the interior of the country. The damage was very substantial at the headquarters of the Ministry of Agriculture. The campus of the national university was under armed siege from dawn until 7 p.m. Throughout the day, constant bursts of machine-gun fire were heard in the university area. The archbishopric intervened to protect people who found themselves caught inside.

On the Hacienda Colima, 18 persons died, at least 15 of whom were peasants. The administrator and the grocer of the ranch also died. The armed forces confirmed that there was a confrontation. A film of the events appreared on TV, and many analyzed interesting aspects of the situation.

At least 50 people died in serious incidents that day: in the capital, seven persons died in the events at the Colonia Santa Lucíá; on the outskirts of Tecnillantas, five people died; and in the area of the trash dump, after the evacuation of that facility by military force, were found the bodies of four workers who had been captured in that action.

Sixteen peasants died in the village of Montepeque, 38 kilometers on the road to Suchitoto. That same day, two students at the University of Central America were captured in Tecnillantas: Mario Nelson and Miguel Alberto Rodríguez Velado, who were brothers. The first one, after four days of illegal detention, was handed over to the courts. Not so for his brother, who was wounded and is still held in illegal detention. Legal Aid is intervening on his behalf.

Amnesty International issued a press release in which it described the repression of the peasants, especially in the area of Chalatenango. The week's events confirm this report in spite of the fact the government denies it. Upon entering the church, I was given a cable that says, "Amnesty International confirmed today (that was yesterday) that in El Salvador human rights are violated to extremes that have not been seen in other countries." That is what Patricio Fuentes (spokesman for the special interest section for Central America in the Swedish Amnesty International) said at a press conference in Managua, Nicaragua.

Fuentes confirmed that, during two weeks of investigations he carried out in El Salvador, he was able to verify 83 political assassinations, between March 10 and 14. He pointed out that Amnesty International, recently condemned by the government of El Salvador, claimed that there had been 600 political assassinations. The Salvadorean government took the opportunity to defend itself against charges, arguing that Amnesty International based its facts on suppositions.

Fuentes said that now we have verified that in El

Salvador human rights are violated to a worse degree than the repression documented in Chile after the coup d'etat. The Salvadorean government also said that the 600 dead were a result of armed confrontations between army troops and guerrillas. Fuentes said that during his stay in El Salvador, he could see that the victims had been tortured before their deaths and mutilated afterwards.

The spokesman of Amnesty International said that the victims' bodies characteristically appeared with the thumbs tied behind their back. Corrosive liquids had been applied to the corpses to prevent identification of the victims by their relatives and to prevent international outcries, the spokesman added. Nevertheless, the bodies were exhumed and the dead have been identified. Fuentes said that the repression wrought by the Salvadorean army will finally destroy the popular organizations through the assassination of leaders in both the city and the country.

According to the spokesman of Amnesty International, at least 3,500 peasants have fled their rural homes to the capital to escape persecution. We have complete lists in London and Sweden of children, youths and women who have been assassinated for trying to organize, affirmed Fuentes.

He said that Amnesty International is a humanitarian organization that does not align itself with governments, organizations or persons. "We do not reject the government, but, yes, we do strive to make human rights respected in every part of the world . . . but especially where they are threatened or trampled down," said Fuentes. Well, this confirms what we have been saying about this frightful week.

I would like to analyze what may be the cause of those violent acts: the work stoppage that the Revolutionary Coordinating Commitee (RCM) called for.

The purpose of the strike is to protest repression. Last Sunday, I said that purpose is legitimate, because it denounces something that cannot be tolerated. But the stoppage also had a political intention, to show that instead of intimidating the popular organizations, the repression was building them up. The intention was to reject opposition from the present government which violently represses people in carrying out its reforms. Some of those reforms, that come under various headings, are not acceptable to the popular organizations.

The state of the country and the misinformation to which we are subject—through official communiques as well as through most of the media—do not yet allow us to measure objectively the extent of the general strike. Foreign broadcasts have reported a 70 percent work stoppage, which would certainly be a very high percentage and could be considered a notable triumph. Not even counting the shops that closed for fear of actions from the left as well as from the right and the government in the early hours of that same Monday, it cannot be denied that the power demonstrated by the RCM in the country, strictly in terms of labor, was great. The RCM was not only strong in the country-side, but also in the factories and in the city.

Very probably the supporters of the RCM committed errors, but in spite of all those failures, it can be judged that that stoppage was an advance in the popular fight and a demonstration that the left can paralyze the economic activity of the country. The government's answer to the stoppage, granted, was hard. Not only did surveillance throughout the city and the wild shooting at the University of El Salvador demonstrate that, but above all the deaths that occurred. No less than ten workers from the factories on strike were killed by agents of the security forces, including three workers from Alcaldia who were assassinated after having been detained by the local police. This is a bad reflection on Alcaldia.

But these deaths were matched by others on the same day, numbering at least 60, according to some people; others say that they surpass 140. Moreover, it is to be noted that the work stoppage was accompanied by the aggressive activities of a few popular organizations. Such is the case in Colima, San Martín and Suchitoto. The tactics of these organizations' operations might be questioned, but their questionableness certainly does not justify the repressive action of the government.

Certainly, the RCM has its faults, and there still remains a lot to be changed in it before it will be a stable alternative for revolutionary democratic power. Would that the RCM might evaluate and perfect its purpose so that it is truly in accord with the wishes of the people.

Then they would not find their wild actions repudiated by the people.

The members of RCM are not failures by being subversive or corrupt or for causing societal resentments: rather, they are failures in that they do not allow normal political development. They are persecuted and massacred; they are hindered in their organizing tasks and in their efforts to expand their relations with other democratic groups. What is going to result is their radicalization and despair. Under these circumstances, it is difficult not to be caught up in revolutionary activities, in aggressive violence. The least that can be said is that the country is experiencing a prerevolutionary stage and in no way a stage of transition.

The fundamental question is how to move along a less violent path at this critical stage. On this point, the greatest responsibility belongs to the civil government, and above all, to the military. How I wish that they would not let themselves be blinded by what they are doing in agrarian reform. That can be a deception that prevents them from seeing the whole problem.

Tuesday—we continue to speak of the past week, a week weighed down by acts that cannot go unmentioned. In the clippings I brought here from the pope, he notes the number of victims that Italy has had during these days, especially in Rome. Well, since the pope pointed out the ten cruel assassinations in Italy, I'm sure if he were in my place, he would take a long time (just as we are taking the time now) to speak of the many, many assassinations that occur here day by day.

On March 18, the bodies of four peasants were found in different areas—two in Metapán, two in San Miguel.

On Wednesday, March 19, at 5:30 a.m., after a military operation in the villages of San Luis La Loma, La Cayetana, León de Piedra, La India, Paz, Opico and El Mono, the bodies of three peasants were found: Humberto Urbino, Oswaldo Hernández and Francisco García.

In the capital at 2 p.m., the premises of both the Trade Union of Beverages and of the Revolutionary Syndicated Federation were occupied by the military. This happened when many workers were keeping watch over the body of Manuel Pacín, consultant for the municipal workers. After having been captured, Pacín was killed: his body was found in Apulo. The military occupation resulted in the deaths of two persons, one of them a worker, Mauricio Batrera, leader of the Union of Industrial Mechanics and Metalworkers.

Nineteen workers were remanded to the courts. At the request of their relatives, Legal Aid is intervening in their defense. It has been confirmed that the union's files were confiscated.

Nine peasants were killed in a confrontation in the town of San Bartolo Tecoluca, as reported in the national press by the armed forces. At noon in the town of El Almendral, in the jurisdiction of Majagual, La Libertad, army soldiers captured three peasants—Miguel Angel Gomez de Paz, Concepción Coralia Menjívar and José Emilio Valencia. They have yet to be freed. We ask that they be handed over to the courts.

At 4 p.m. on Thursday, March 20, in the village of El Jocote, Quezaltepeque, a peasant leader named Alfonso Muñoz Pacheco was assassinated. The strike secretary for the Federation of Rural Workers, peasant Muñoz was known widely in the country for his dedication to the cause of the peasants.

And something very terrible, very important happened on this same day (Thursday, March 20)— Agustín Sánchez, a peasant, was found still alive but critically wounded. On March 15, he had been captured in Zacatecoluca by soldiers who handed him over to the local police. Peasant Sánchez has affirmed, in a declaration given before a notary and witnesses, that his capture occurred on the ranch of El Cauca, in the district of La Paz, where he was working in connection with the Salvadorean Common Union.

The police detained him for four days, without food and water, torturing him with constant whippings and throttlings until March 19, when they shot him and two other peasants in the head. Luckily, the bullet only shattered his right cheekbone and eye. Found dying in the early morning, he was helped by some peasants until a reliable person took him to this capital. Peasant Sánchez could not sign this horrid testimony because they had smashed both of his hands. Persons known to be honorable witnessed his horrible conditions, and there are photographs that reveal the state in which this poor peasant was picked up.

In San Pablo Tacachico, we have a report, as yet unconfirmed, of the mass murder of 25 peasants. At the beginning of this mass, we received confirmation of this terrible tragedy. The report says that on March 21 from 6 a.m. on, a military operation took place on Santa Ana Street, which runs through San Pablo Tacachico. The operation mentioned was carried out by soldiers from the Opico and Santa Ana quarters, along with the security guards assigned to Tacachico. They carried with them secret lists of names of persons to be searched.

In the operation mentioned, the soldiers and police carried out a search in the villages of El Resbaladero, San Felipe, Moncagua, El Portillo, San José La Cova, Mogotes, and their respective settlements, Los Pozos and Las Delicias. The soldiers and police also searched all who were riding by bus or walking on foot.

In the village of Mogotes, in the jurisdiction of Tacachico, the repression was most cruel, as the troops of soldiers, with two small tanks, spread terror among the inhabitants of this sector. In the search they carried out, four radios and 400 colónes in hard cash were stolen. The troops burned the home and all of the belongings of Rosalio Cruz, whom they have left, along with his family, in the worse misery.

They assassinated Alejandro Mojica and Félix Santos; Mojica was killed in his own house and Santos was killed in a dry river bed. Both left wives and children as orphans. For fear of repression, they were buried on their own land, but their bodies were removed without the knowledge of Isabel Cruz, Manuel Santos and Santos Urquilla.

A final tragedy occurred this week: yesterday afternoon, UCA (the University of Central America) was attacked for the first time and without any provocation. We want to express a special solidarity with the victims and the school. A full brigade from the national police started this operation at 1:15 p.m. They entered the campus shooting. One student who was found studying mathematics was assassinated. His name was Manuel Orantes Guillén.

People tell me that various students have disappeared and that their relatives and the UCA are protesting their disappearance through the peaceful negotiations of a countryman, who should be respected for his autonomy. What they have not done at the national university, no doubt because of fear, they have done at UCA, which is not armed to defend itself—a fact showing that it has been attacked without provocation. We hope to give more details of this, which is a serious offense against the civilized spirit and against the laws of our country.

Let us think for a moment about the meaning of these months. Beloved brothers and sisters, I do not want to take more of your time, but it would be interesting now to analyze what these months have meant to a new government that clearly would like to pull us out of these horrid situations. And yet if what it aims for is to cut down the leaders of the people's organization and impede the process which the people want, then it cannot advance along another path. Without being rooted in the people, no government can be effective. Any government will be far from effective if it wants to implant its own roots in the country with the force of blood and suffering.

I would like to issue a special entreaty to the members of the army, and specifically to the ranks of the National Guard, the police and the military. Brothers and sisters, you are our own people; you kill your own fellow peasants. Someone's order to kill should not prevail; rather, what ought to prevail is the law of God that says, "Do not kill." No soldier is obliged to obey an order against the law of God; no one has to fulfill an immoral law. There is still time for you to follow your conscience, even in the face of the sinful order to kill.

The church, defender of the rights of God, of God's law, of the dignity of the human being, of the person, cannot keep quiet before such abhorrent action. We want the government to take seriously the fact that its reforms are of no service if they continue to leave the people so bloodied. Why, in the name of God, and in the name of this suffering people whose cries rise up to the heavens every day in greater tumult, I implore them, I beg them, I order them, in the name of God: Cease the repression!

The church preaches your liberation just as we have studied it in the holy Bible today. It is a liberation that has, above all else, respect for the dignity of the person, hope for humanity's common good, and the transcendency that looks before all to God and only from God derives its hope and its strength.

Let us now proclaim our faith in that truth.

March 24, 1980
# In Death Is Our LIfe

*This was the last homily of Archbishop Oscar A. Romero, given at 5 p.m. in the chapel at Divine Providence Hospital in San Salvador.*

Through our various dealings with the publishing house of the newspaper *El Independiente*, I have been able to observe the filial sentiments of Doña Sara's children on the anniversary of their mother's death. Above all, I have seen the noble spirit that belonged to dear Doña Sara, who placed all her education and intelligence at the service of a cause that is so vital today: the true liberation of our people.

This afternoon, I believe that her brothers and sisters should not only pray for the eternal rest of their dear deceased one, but should especially heed her message, one that every Christian must live intensely. Many surprise us by thinking that Christianity should not meddle in these things, but our duty is the exact opposite.

We have just heard in the Lord's gospel that we must

not love ourselves more than him, that we must not refrain from plunging into those risks history demands
of us, and that those wanting to separate themselves
from danger will lose their lives. On the other hand,
those who surrender to the service of people through
love of Christ will live like the grain of wheat that dies.
It only apparently dies. If it were not to die, it would
remain a solitary grain. The harvest comes because the
grain of wheat dies. The earth is also left to die, to break
up, because only by undoing itself does it produce the
harvest.

I have chosen an excerpt from a Vatican II document
that applies to dear Doña Sara now in heaven. It says
this: "We know neither the moment of the consumma-
tion of the earth and of humanity nor the way the uni-
verse will be transformed. The form of this world, distorted by sin, is passing away and we are taught that
God is preparing a new dwelling and a new earth in
which righteousness dwells, whose happiness will fill
and surpass all the desires of peace arising in human
hearts. Then with death conquered God's children will
be raised in Christ and what was sown in weakness and
dishonor will put on the imperishable: charity and its
works will remain and all of creation, which God made
for human beings, will be set free from its bondage to
decay."

We know that winning the whole world does not
matter if we lose ourselves. The expectation of a new
earth—the preoccupation with perfecting this earth,
where the human race grows anew, already gives us a
glimpse of the new world—should not deaden us, but

rather enliven us. We must distinguish carefully between temporal progress and the kingdom of Christ. Nevertheless, if temporal progress contributes to ordering human society better, then temporal progress concerns the reign of God to a great extent.

When we have spread human dignity, unity and freedom—in a word, all the excellent fruits of nature and our effort—throughout the earth in the spirit of the Lord and in accord with his command, we will find that, when Christ surrenders the eternal and universal kingdom to the Father, human nature will be free of all stain, illuminated and transformed. "His kingdom will be a kingdom of truth and life, the realm of holiness and grace; a kingdom of justice, love and peace." The kingdom is already mysteriously present on our earth; when the Lord comes, he will perfect his creation.

This hope comforts us as Christians. We know that every effort to improve society, above all when society is so full of injustice and sin, is an effort that God blesses, that God wants, that God demands of us. And when one meets noble people like Doña Sarita, and sees her thinking embodied in little Jorge and in all those who work for these ideals, one must try to purify these ideals for Christianity, yes, to wrap them in hope for what is beyond. Our good deeds are stronger if done with faith. We have the security of knowing that what we plant on earth, if we nourish it with Christian hope, will never fail; we will find our efforts purified in that kingdom where merit clearly lies in what we have done on this earth.

I believe that it would be vain to aspire to great visions of hope and struggle on this anniversary. We simply and gratefully remember this noble woman who understood the restlessness of her son and of all who work for a better world, who knew as well how to plant her share of wheat grain in the suffering of the people. There is no doubt that Doña Sara's self-giving is the guarantee that her reward is heaven, the reward that must come for making the sacrifice and showing the understanding that many need at this moment in El Salvador.

I implore all of you, beloved brothers and sisters, to seek a better world from an historical vantage point, to have hope, joined with a spirit of surrender and sacrifice. We must do what we can. All of us can do something. First, from the outset, we must have a sense of understanding. Maybe this blessed woman that we are remembering today could not do things directly, but she inspired those who could by understanding their struggle, and above all, by praying.

And even after her death, she lives on and says from eternity that it is worth the effort to work for the kingdom. If we illuminate with Christian hope those longings for justice, peace and goodness that we still have on this earth, they will be realized. Those who have put into their work a feeling of great faith, of love for God, of hope for humanity, find all that work now overflowing in the splendors of a crown. Such has been the reward for all of those who do that work, watering the earth with truth, justice, love and kindness. These deeds are not lost; purified by the spirit of God, their effects are our reward.

This holy mass, this eucharist is clearly an act of faith. Our Christian faith shows us that in this moment contention is changed into the body of the Lord who offers himself for the redemption of the world. In the chalice, the wine is transformed into the blood that was the price of salvation. This body broken and this blood shed for human beings encourage us to give our body and blood up to suffering and pain, as Christ did —not for self, but to bring justice and peace to our people. Let us be intimately united, then, in faith and hope at this moment of prayer for dear Doña Sara and for ourselves.

*At this point, Archbishop Romero was shot to death.*

# Afterword

## Rev. Virgil Elizondo
*Director, Mexican-American Cultural Center*

In moments of great suffering and crisis, God has always raised great prophets among us to straighten the ways of humanity, to call it to repent from its evil ways and to return to God's way of truth and love before global disaster befalls us all. The prophetic voice has never come from among the officialdom, the mighty or the wise of this world. Out of unsuspected places God calls simple and unassuming persons to confront the sin of the world with the power of prophetic truth— the truth about humanity which needs no proof or clarification. It is self-evident both to those who are suffering and dying and to those who perpetuate the lies of the world in order to mask the evil ways which allow their own crimes to appear as virtue while making their victims appear as public sinners and enemies of law and order.

In our own day and time, out of a small and relatively unknown country of the world, El Salvador, God has raised a great prophet in the person of Archbishop

Oscar Romero. It was my privilege to know the Arch-bishop very briefly on a few occasions. The last time was during the Puebla conference of 1979. He was a simple and unassuming pastor. His whole person radiated kindness and compassion. His eyes exhibited a deep suffering coupled with the brilliance of joyful expectation. As the reporters from around the world corralled him tightly and bombarded him with questions, he tried in a very calm way to answer each one in clear and precise terms. He always had a warm smile on his face, never expressing anger or vengeance, yet clearly pointing out with unquestioned clarity and certitude the real sources of evil which were destroying his people and condemning them to a perpetual life of misery and suffering. Truly he was a man of God. Because he was alive with God's life which is love unlimited, he was not afraid to face death for the sake of life. His beautiful saying—*Si me matan resucitare en las luchas de mi pueblo,* "If they kill me I will resurrect in the struggles of my people"—brings out the profound faith and love of this man who knew that even if they killed him he would not die.

The homilies of Archbishop Romero are not political or economic discourses. Neither are they mere commentaries on the holy scriptures of old—*in illo tempore.* They are truly, in the style of the great fathers of the church, actualizations of God's words today. God is truly present in the midst of our sinful situation. From the concrete and very particular situation of each day, this man of faith goes to the scriptures which the church reads on that particular day so that God's word may bring out clearly the ways of God operating and effective in the lives of the people. It is through the example of the young, poor country priest killed for defending his youth club that the Archbishop retells the story of death and resurrection. It is through the common work and struggles of the people that the Archbishop retells the meaning of the Christian pilgrimage. As Jesus did, so does the Archbishop. He takes the simple and the ordinary stuff of everyday life and through it brings out God's plan and project for humanity.

His homilies are long, yet they seem very brief because they are full of newness and realism. They are creative and dynamic. They do not just speak about the gospel, but they are the gospel—the good news about salvation in the very moment when we are perishing. One atheist in El Salvador stated, "I am not a Christian but I listen to him because he is the only one who has something to say." His words are reminiscent of the confession of the centurion, "Truly this is a just man."

The homilies are packed. They are good theology, good spiritual meditation, good catechesis, good homilies and excellent commentaries on the ultimate meaning of the daily news. Read them many times, for each time you will be enriched and challenged. You will share in the suffering yet you will equally share in the joyful expectation of the great dream that is already beginning to come to life.

For us in the United States they have a very special relevance. They are the collective voice of the powerless, the voiceless and the poor of the world speaking to the president of our country, to our government officials, to our business people and most of all to each one of us. The poverty and misery of these peoples are condemnation to the rich of the world. We the people of the United States and the people of the Western, technological and industrialized countries are the rich of the world. As John Paul II said at Yankee Stadium, the gap between Lazarus and the rich man is growing into a gigantic abyss. The rich man refused to listen to Lazarus. Will we too refuse to listen to God's prophets who come from the side of Lazarus? It is not easy for the rich to enter the kingdom of heaven. The gospel is quite clear on this point. Will we, the rich and the industrial peoples of the West, listen to our own worldly wisdom or will we listen to God's prophets? Or will we continue to destroy them so that we won't have to listen to them and in so doing ensure our own ultimate destruction? There is no doubt that materialism, individualism, consumerism, and upward mobility without limits are destroying us from within as a people. Our commercial conglomerates depersonalize the exploitation of resources and persons so that the average American is not even aware of our oppression of the masses of poor people of the world. We, as a people, are responsible but because we are blind to the global aspects of the situation, we are not even aware of what we are doing. The masses of our American people are good people but we are too deeply entrapped in the collective blindness of egoism of our consumer society. We need to break through so that we ourselves might see and be liberated from the prisons we have built for ourselves that continue to make ultimate salvation impossible. The voice of Archbishop Romero calls us to profound *metanoia* not just of the individual but even of the collective person we are as United States and as Western civilization.

In this small and insignificant man, God speaks to us in our day. He invites us, he challenges us, he offers us hope. His message is not sophisticated or difficult to understand. It is as ordinary and as extraordinary as the gospel itself. We can present it. We can only hope and pray many will hear it and through it gain true evangelical insight; may we truly see reality as it really is and be able to denounce sin in its concrete and social dimension; may we in turn begin to live and announce the kingdom of God for all men and women of today.

The voice of Oscar Romero calls all of us to profound conversion to the ways of the gospel. It does not call for insurrection, but invites us and even challenges us to die to our selfish selves and find resurrection.

Out of El Salvador, a contemporary savior calls us to salvation. Like the original one, he was killed by the powers of this world. But he is not dead. He is alive in the struggles of all Christians who work to build a more human civilization.

Also available from
## Celebration Books

# To Comfort
# All Who Mourn

## Carol Luebering

Based on her personal experience in a Cincinnati parish, Carol Luebering shows how any church can start a ministry to the grieving. She describes the practical helps, liturgical assistance and long-term support the community can give to its bereaved. Luebering has served on her parish liturgy committee and the Cincinnati Archdiocesan Worship Commission.
Soft-cover.

ISBN 0-934134-07-3, 96 pages, $4.95

Celebration Books, P.O. Box 281, Kansas City, MO 64141

Also available from

# Celebration Books

# Reassessing

## Arthur Jones

Using the rosary as a way of patterning the mind, journalist Arthur Jones replaces the traditional "mysteries" with reflections on the realities of contemporary Christian life to find a vocabulary for individual piety. A vigorous, vital evaluation of the material things in our lives, and a fresh way of looking at our relationships with other people.
Soft-cover.

ISBN 0-934134-05-7, 100 pages, $3.50

Celebration Books, P.O. Box 281, Kansas City, MO 64141

Also available from
# Celebration Books

# The Illustrated Sunday

This book contains 198 drawings by 27 artists in a variety of styles. The contents are arranged in sequence according to the order of the three-year liturgical cycle. Handy indexes list the scripture verses depicted by the drawings and their appropriate use for other celebrations beyond the Sunday liturgy.
Soft-cover.

ISBN 0-934134-04-9, 88 pages, $5.95

Celebration Books, P.O. Box 281, Kansas City, MO 64141

Also available from

## Celebration Books

# The Year
# of Luke

## Eugene LaVerdiere

Scripture scholar Father LaVerdiere applies his skills to the Bible texts assigned for Sundays and holydays in the C cycle (1980, 1983, 1986, etc.). A fresh interpretation of God's word for homilists, liturgy planners and individuals who want to deepen their appreciation of the Sunday scriptures.
Soft-cover.

ISBN 0-934134-01-4, 200 pages, $6.95

Celebration Books, P.O. Box 281, Kansas City, MO 64141

Also available from

# Celebration Books

# Loving and Dying

## Donald Senior

Scripture scholar Donald Senior offers a popular commentary on the lectionary texts for weddings and funerals for homilists who must preach to Christians about loving and dying. His book is also a must for engaged couples planning their wedding liturgy and for mourning families who look to the scripture in faith and hope.
Soft-cover.

ISBN 0-934134-00-6, 88 pages, $2.95

Celebration Books, P.O. Box 281, Kansas City, MO 64141

Also available from
## Celebration Books

# Introduction to Parish Liturgy

## Gordon E. Truitt

The perfect handbook for clergy, liturgical ministers and liturgy committee members. Father Truitt, former chairman of the Federation of Diocesan Liturgical Commissions, synthesizes the liturgical reform of the past 15 years and presents a deeper spiritual understanding of the rites now celebrated in parishes. Soft-cover.

ISBN 0-934134-02-2, 56 pages, $2.95

Celebration Books, P.O. Box 281, Kansas City, MO 64141

Also available from

# Celebration Books

# The Once and Future Church

## Barbara O'Dea

The Rite of Christian Initiation of Adults contains a vision of the church that must come to life in every parish. Barbara O'Dea, Director of Liturgy for the Diocese of Pueblo, describes the obstacles to that vision and shows how local churches can overcome them. The Rite of Christian Initiation, she says, is for the whole parish, not just for its new members.

Soft-cover.

ISBN 0-934134-08-1, 96 pages, $4.95

Celebration Books, P.O. Box 281, Kansas City, MO 64141